LANGUAGE PROCESSING PROBLEMS

LANGUAGE PROCESSING PROBLEMS

A Guide for Parents and Teachers

Cindy Gaulin

ISBN #:   Softcover   0-7388-5552-9

This book was printed in the United States of America.

To order additional copies of this book, contact:
Xlibris Corporation
1-888-7-XLIBRIS
www.Xlibris.com
Orders@Xlibris.com

CONTENTS

1: Introduction 9

2: Background 14

 What is language processing? *14*

 How we use speech to communicate *15*

 Research into language processing *17*

3: Components of language processing 20

 Language knowledge and language processing *20*

 Word recognition *21*

 Working memory *22*

 Bottom-up and top-down processing *25*

4: Modes of language processing 29

 Input processing and output processing *29*

 Auditory and visual language processing *30*

5: How do children learn to process language? 33

6: Problems with language processing 36

 Defining the problem *36*

 What causes language processing problems? *41*

7: Confusions of terminology 44

 What's in a name? *44*

 Severity *45*

8: Intrinsic factors related to LPP 47

 Intelligence *47*

 Attention Deficit Disorder *49*

 Language Learning Disability and Specific Language
  Impairment *50*

 Auditory temporal processing deficit *52*

 Phonological processing problem *53*

 Other neurological impairments *54*

 Dyslexia *55*

9: Extrinsic factors related to LPP 56

 Sensory deprivation *56*

 Middle ear disease *57*

 Institutionalization *58*

10: Summarizing language processing problems 60

11: Does my child have a language processing problem? 62

   Recognizing LPP in preschoolers *63*

   Recognizing LPP in school-age children *68*

   Recognizing LPP in high school students *74*

12: What if my child has a language processing problem? 78

   Getting an evaluation *78*

   Tests of language processing *81*

   Do children with LPP need special services? *84*

13: How Can I Help? 87

14: Suggestions for improving listening and following directions 90

   External strategies *90*

   Internal strategies *93*

   The speech-language pathologist's role in improving

      listening and following directions. *94*

15: Suggestions for improving verbal memory 97

   External strategies *97*

   Internal strategies *100*

   The speech-language pathologist's role in improving

      verbal memory. *101*

16:Suggestions for improving word retrieval 103

   External strategies *103*

   Internal strategies *104*

   The speech-language pathologist's role in improving

      word retrieval. *105*

17: Suggestions for improving organization of

  language output 106

   External strategies *106*

   Internal strategies *107*

   The speech-language pathologist's role in improving

      organization of language output. *108*

18: A final word 111

GLOSSARY 113

WORKS CITED 117

To the children, their parents and teachers who have made this happen. And with special thanks to Steve, Tom, Charlotte, Susan and Merrilee.

1

INTRODUCTION

Mandy is nine years old. She is an intelligent and artistic little girl who enjoys school. During class discussions she is alert and seems to be bursting with information to share. But when called on she has trouble answering. She fidgets, repeats herself and can't seem to find the right words. She uses some gestures to help get her point across, but in the end she may just shrug, saying "You know what I mean".

Five-year-old Ryan is cheerful and sociable. But since starting kindergarten he has been having a hard time adjusting to school demands. Often he doesn't know what he is supposed to do. And he gets in trouble because he talks when he should be listening.

At 15, Jay is a hard worker in school but very quiet. He has a few good friends but is not gregarious. He prefers running track to playing on the baseball team. He gets decent grades except in math. He also complains that it is hard to keep up when taking notes in history class.

Since she began talking her parents have always considered Beth to be brilliant. She has a huge vocabulary and at age four she can already read some simple sentences. True, Beth seems to have her head in the clouds, at times, forgetting the names of common objects and sometimes giving very unusual answers to questions. And she does have a temper, often throwing a tantrum in the worst possible situations. Now that she is in preschool she often seems confused and is becoming withdrawn. Her parents and teachers are worried.

What do these children have in common? Each one of them has a language processing problem which is interfering with some aspects of social and/or academic development. To begin to understand the problems these children have we need to take some time to find out more about how we communicate and what can go wrong with the process.

Being able to communicate by speaking is an incredible ability. It lets us tell others what we need and how we feel. With language we can share information and interact with other humans for any purpose we choose. We often take our spoken communication for granted. After all, almost everyone can talk. We are delighted when our infant begins to use words but we are not really surprised. Normal children are expected to learn to speak and understand language.

Because of this expectation, parents are surprised to learn that a good number of children do not develop speech and language as an easy natural process. A broad range of problems can interfere with language development. Among other things they include hearing impairment, delay in overall development and stroke or other neurological damage occurring before, during or just after birth. And surprisingly, there are quite a number of children who seem to have no clear reason for their difficulty. Fortunately, most children with serious problems which could interfere with language development are identified quite early and they can begin to receive appropriate treatment for their problems. Even those children who do not exhibit impairments in infancy are usually identified by two or three years of age because they are not learning to use language as expected. And then they, too, can begin to receive speech and language therapy to address their specific problems.

However, over and above the children who have readily observable speech and language problems, there is still a group of children who have difficulty with language, but whose problems are hidden. The problems are hidden because what parents observe doesn't seem to be related to the child's language skills. If your child can talk and understand what you say and knows plenty of words, you generally assume that his language is normal. If he doesn't always listen or gets confused or has trouble making friends you are concerned, but it is unlikely that you would attribute these problems to language. If the teacher tells you your child has a tremendous vocabulary, why would you imagine that her difficulties with math might be due to language problems?

The reason hidden language problems are usually overlooked is because our impressions of a person's language skill are often based on the meaning they convey rather than on how their meaning is expressed. Thus, both casual observation and standardized language tests usually assess a child's knowledge of vocabulary and grammar. The other side of the language coin is the facility we have to use what we know about language to speak and understand effectively in a variety of situations. This facility is called language processing. The efficiency with which we process language varies. And this variable ability depends on factors such as how we feel and what is going on around us. Language processing can, thus, appear inconsistent and problems can be difficult to pin down.

Spoken language is used by people of all ages and language processing problems can occur at any age. While the information contained in this book will be helpful in understanding the language processing impairments of individuals of any age, it is aimed particularly at the language processing problems encountered by children and young people. My interest in the language processing problems of children has been a direct outgrowth of my clinical work as a pediatric speech-language pathologist. It is also based on my own experiences as a child with mild, but annoying, problems processing language.

This book is my response to the frustration I have seen in children and their parents and teachers when language processing difficulties cause communication breakdown, confusion and behavior problems. Frequently, improvement in communication and attitude begins as soon as parents, teachers and children themselves understand the problem and how to attack it. I hope this book answers the questions you may have about language processing in your own child and in the children you know. And I hope it will provide the information you need to make communication more pleasant and effective.

Because my work has been with children I am particularly interested in and sensitive to the process of language learning. For this reason, the book also addresses the intimate connection between language learning and language processing.

In chapters 1 and 2 of the book you will find a brief and nontechnical overview of the communication process and what researchers have discovered about how our brains normally process language. In order to help you understand various language processing problems chapters 3 and 4 describe the components and modes of language processing. And chapter 5 deals with how children learn to process language.

In chapter 6 we begin to explore the kinds of problems people can have with language processing. Chapter 7 helps to sort out some confusions of terminology that have arisen in the areas of language and auditory processing. Chapters 8 and 9 deal with individual and environmental factors that relate to language processing problems and explore the similarities and differences between language processing problems and a number of related disorders. Chapter 10 summarizes the kinds of problems children have with language processing and touches on the complex interaction between the type and severity of the problem and the child's strengths and weaknesses in other areas.

Chapter 11 provides information to help you recognize the signs of language processing difficulty in your child. This chapter will help you see how apparently unrelated behaviors at home, at school and at play may be attributable to difficulties processing language. In chapter 12 information is provided about getting a professional evaluation of your child's language processing ability and about various possible treatment plans. Chapter 13 provides general guidelines about what parents and teachers can do to help.

Finally, chapters 14 through 17 give specific ideas about what you can do to make language interactions go more smoothly. There are many suggestions that parents and teachers can try. In addition there are suggestions that will help your child take an active part in improving his or her communicative interactions and school performance. In each of these four chapters there is also information about the kinds of treatment a speech-language pathologist could provide for your child.

2
BACKGROUND

What is language processing?

Have you ever been in a situation when you didn't understand what people were talking about? Perhaps you turned on a movie in the middle or joined a group at a party just as the punch line of a joke was delivered. Or maybe you found yourself in a lecture on astrophysics when you thought it was going to be about gardening. In each of these cases you surely had trouble getting the point. In our daily lives we constantly interpret incoming information and we usually do it very efficiently, but these examples indicate that all of us sometimes have difficulties making sense of what we are hearing. Missing information is the main reason for processing problems. In the previous examples it is clear why information is missing, but in reality there are many less obvious reasons why language input might not be effectively perceived or processed.

We normally use language so easily that we are unaware that we are doing something very complicated. It is only when we look closely at what is involved in listening and talking that we begin to realize what amazing abilities we have. In fact, understanding and producing spoken language are among the most complex things humans do. An incredible amount and variety of information has to be dealt with in any spoken exchange. Many steps are involved in understanding and responding to messages. Fortunately, communication happens quite rapidly and automatically, that is, without our awareness of what is being accomplished.

The automatic work that transforms the sounds of language

into meaning when we listen and that transforms our meanings into ordered sounds when we speak is called language processing. The complexity of language processing means that it is prone to interference and breakdown. Luckily, for most speakers the problems are mild and temporary, but more severe and permanent difficulties do occur.

Understanding how the human brain handles spoken language can give us insight into sources of confusion, misunderstanding, and sometimes inexplicable behavior in others. Why do some children have trouble following directions? Why are some children made fun of more than others? Why does a child who is talkative at home become shy and tongue-tied in a group? What about the child who can do division some days but not others? Each of these children may be suffering from a language processing problem that has not been detected.

An understanding of language processing can also teach us something about effort, creativity and resourcefulness. Many children work doubly hard to learn in spite of significant trouble processing language. Others invent ways to succeed at learning when the ways they are taught don't work.

As we take a closer look at how we use language to communicate, I hope you will begin to share my feelings of awe at what each child must accomplish in order to join our speaking society. Each time I evaluate a child and get to know how he processes language, I feel I have made an intimate connection with that child's intellect. I see a little glimmer of who that child is. Each child brings his physical and mental endowments and his experiences to bear on the problem of learning to use language. The problem-solving strategies children use in this endeavor are many, varied and worthy of our interest.

How we use speech to communicate

When we listen to speech we "hear" words. But actually the sounds being produced by a speaker are not divided into words.

Speakers produce a continuous stream of sound. What is actually happening is that the air in front of the speaker's mouth is being moved in waves. The pattern of the waves is determined by the stream of breath as it is varied by movements of the speaker's tongue and lips and the changing shape of his oral cavity. If we did not have ears specifically tuned to the shape and size of these waves we would only detect speech as mouth movements and a warm breeze emanating from a speaker's mouth. However, just as a radio or television receiver is specifically tuned to the frequencies and amplitudes of broadcast signals, our ears are well tuned to the frequencies and amplitudes of human speech.

A speaker produces a continuous stream of sounds and our ears can pick up the signal. But it is our brain which analyzes the signal by breaking the stream into words. We can then make sense of the message using information we already know about language.

Every language has three basic components; a set of sounds, words made from those sounds and a system for combining words to convey meaning. Thus, language is a set of codes. The speech sounds (phonemes) are bits of code that can be arranged in various ways to form words. Words are also code. A word is an arbitrary sequence of phonemes that stands for a concept. As we learn language, we learn the meanings that speakers of our language associate with a particular word. In addition to knowing what words mean, our ability to understand a sentence depends on our being able to figure out the relationship between words. To comprehend what we hear, our brains compute these grammatical relationships so we can tell who did what to whom. For example, the analysis will tell us whether the dog bit the man or the man bit the dog.

Understanding language requires us to recognize the elements of the codes and know the rules for combining them. If we want to utter our thoughts, we must also be able to use the codes and rules to plan and execute the many rapid muscle movements involved in speech production. Above and beyond all these mechanics of speech and language, a speaker has to make sure that she conveys the message she intends and that it is appropriate for the listener and the situation. Thus, language is an incredibly complicated set of codes and rules that must be used simultaneously and interdependently. How do we manage to do it without even noticing how hard it is?

This question can be answered on at least two levels. First of all, our brains must be designed to do it. Second, we have had a lot of practice. The ability to use language effectively normally increases with age. This is due to learning, practice and the automaticity that comes from repeated use. Automaticity means that something we have done many times no longer requires our conscious attention to complete. From infancy we learn, use and integrate basic information about language. Our brains are structured such that this repetition and practice result in dedicated pathways for language analysis. Thus we no longer need to pay attention to those processes. Most aspects of language are analyzed automatically and simultaneously while our conscious attention addresses the meaning of the message.

Research into language processing

Scientists and philosophers have been studying language for as long as we know. But until relatively recently the focus of study was mainly on the content and structure of language rather than on the details of how we process linguistic information. During the 1950's researchers began grappling with the problem of getting computers to understand speech. Their early research met with little success, but it spurred further study of the brain's ability to perceive, store and use spoken language. Since the 1950's psychologists and other researchers have undertaken tens of thousands of studies addressing aspects of language processing. Because they study how the brain uses language these scientists are called psycholinguists. They have been developing models of what might be taking place in our brains when we listen to, understand and respond to language.

The information processing that takes place during speaking

and listening is often referred to as on-line language processing, because it is happening right at the same time we are trying to communicate. Research into on-line language processing has provided a wealth of detail. Some psycholinguists focus on how the brain perceives and interprets speech sounds. Others are concerned with how ideas are stored as words and later retrieved in a form we can use to produce speech. There has also been much research into how word meaning, sentence structure and context affect our understanding of sentences. The results of these studies have added tremendously to our understanding of language processing.

The initial studies of language processing were conducted with adults. Some early researchers constructed sentences which, while completely grammatical, led listeners to jump to the wrong conclusions. These sentences were called "garden path" sentences because they tended to lead the listener astray. The most famous example is the sentence "The horse raced past the barn fell." We don't expect to hear the word "fell" at the end of this sentence and aren't really ready to understand the meaning of the final form of the sentence. However, in English it is possible, grammatically, to shorten sentences like "The horse that was raced past the barn fell" to "The horse raced past the barn fell". Occasionally this results in garden path sentences. In such cases features of the vocabulary and structure of English interfere with processing. Other studies looked not at how language structure can cause misunderstandings, but how neurons in our brains can misfire and produce unusual results. Slips of the tongue and reversals of sounds or words are common examples. This last type of error can produce some very funny statements such as "He disarmed the bandits in one swell foop". We call these reversals "Spoonerisms" after the Reverend W.A. Spooner, a British clergyman and professor who was famous for them. One of his most famous slips was rising at High Table to propose a toast to the "Dear Old Queen". You can work out the result.

Other researchers wanted to know what could be learned about language processing from patients who had language impairments due to stroke or other brain damage. Studies comparing the performance of adults with normal language ability and language-impaired adults provided worthwhile information for developing theories about mature language processing. And the results were useful in developing therapies for adults who had lost some of their language processing abilities.

But language development is different from mature language use. Likewise, children who have difficulty learning to use language are different from adults who once used language normally and lost that ability due to illness or injury. Thus it is often difficult to make inferences about children's language processing from the original studies of adults.

Fortunately, in recent years more studies have addressed language processing in children. Most of these studies have compared normal children and children with language impairments. Little by little, results from these studies are being integrated into educational and therapeutic programs. But it takes time to discover what strategies and therapies work best with which children. Thus there is often a significant lag before the practical applications of research findings become generally available. The research continues for there is still a lot to learn. But the time is overdue for parents and teachers to have some basic information about children's language processing.

3

COMPONENTS OF LANGUAGE PROCESSING

Our brain stores all the information we have about language and it also does all the processing. Although we don't yet understand exactly how it does all this, researchers have described some specific routines the brain uses to make sense of language. In this chapter we will examine some of the processes which enable us to use language so effectively.

Language knowledge and language processing

Before going much further I should draw a clear distinction between language knowledge and language processing. In a sense this seems easy to do, but reflection reveals that the two are closely intertwined. I want to try to separate the concepts because differences in performance in the two areas are important in diagnosing language processing disorders.

Language knowledge is what you know about language. It includes your knowledge of the sounds, words and grammar of your language. It allows you to judge whether something is a word, whether it is being pronounced correctly, whether a sentence is grammatical and even what things are okay to say to whom.

In contrast, language processing refers to the ability to efficiently manage various kinds of language information. Processing comprises the chain of events that begins with perception of sensory input, in the case of spoken language, through hearing. It entails decoding and recoding information from one form to another. For example, as we learned earlier, auditory signals start as sound waves. These waves vibrate the eardrums (tympanic membrane) in a specific pattern. That pattern of movement is mechanically transferred to the inner ear (cochlea) by the movement of a series of small bones. In the cochlea the movement pattern is translated into electrical impulses in the form of nerve-cell (neuron) firing. These electrical impulses activate specific patterns of neurons in the cortex of the brain. The cortex is the part of the brain where messages from all parts of the brain finally meet and become integrated for use and storage. The patterns of nerve firing based on the new sound waves coming into our ears are compared with existing patterns (i.e., words) already stored in the cortex from previous experience. All of these complex processes are taking place at a level below our conscious awareness. When a match is found, the word and the idea expressed come to the surface of our awareness. What happens before that point, however, is pretty much out of our conscious control.

Word recognition

There are differing theories about how our brains divide the speech stream and recognize words. Some researchers hypothesize that the brain can divide what we hear immediately into recognizable whole words, while others claim that individual sounds are the unit of analysis. Most current theories hypothesize large numbers of comparisons taking place simultaneously. According to one popular model, word recognition takes place by a process of elimination. The first information about a word that reaches the brain activates all the possible words beginning the same way. As further information arrives the field of alternatives is narrowed and the number of potential words is reduced.

By analogy we might think about the old game of "Name that Tune". When given the first note of a song, in isolation, it is difficult or impossible to recognize the song. There are many songs which begin with the same note. But as more notes are heard the possibilities dramatically decline and we often know after only a few notes what the song is. So it is with language. Words can often be recognized or sentences understood before all the sensory information is received. Automatic analysis of incoming information is performed at the word, sentence and message level simultaneously. As comparisons with stored information take place, the meaning of the message emerges in a form which our conscious mind can understand. All of this happens extremely quickly. It takes about 200 milliseconds (one fifth of a second) for an adult to recognize a one-syllable word in the context of a sentence.

What actually happens in the brain is still mostly a mystery. The physical makeup of our thoughts is poorly understood. Fortunately, we can recognize language processing problems without having to plumb those depths. One thing we do know is that language processing depends critically on memory.

Working memory

Memory span is a term used to describe how many words or digits a person can remember. Memory span has been studied for a long time and is sometimes referred to as short-term memory. Memory span is what allows you to remember a new telephone number until you dial it or a short shopping list until you get to the store. You may be aware of repeating the items to yourself in the interim. At one time it was determined the average adult's short-term memory could hold about 7 words or digits. But it turns out that this view of short-term memory as a place to hold a list of words is too static. Short-term memory is a more dynamic part of our thinking and learning abilities.

Some years ago, Alan Baddeley and his colleagues decided to find out what short-term memory was for. They carried out a series of elegant experiments which showed how short-term memory interacted with the cognitive processes of comprehension, reasoning and learning. In general these experiments took the following form. Subjects were asked to keep remembering a list of digits at the same time they were doing another cognitive task. It was found that all the main language-based cognitive functions (comprehension, verbal reasoning and verbal learning) were somewhat impaired, but not obliterated, by rehearsal of a list of 7 or 8 digits, but that rehearsal of only 3 digits did not interfere much at all with these operations. These results indicate that comprehension, reasoning and learning depend on the same system as short-term recall. This finding led to the development of a multi-component model of short-term memory which was termed "working memory".

Working memory emphasizes the integrative function of the system rather than reflecting a static memory capacity. Various researchers have studied working memory and proposed models of how it works. The models typically ascribe to working memory the functions of processing and storage of information. The research of Marcel Just and Patricia Carpenter has highlighted the important point that working memory systems are of limited capacity. They have found that individuals vary in their working memory capacity and that limitations on working memory capacity are associated with greater difficulty with language comprehension.

Baddeley has developed a model of working memory which includes a central executive that controls at least two separate subsystems. The two well-studied subsystems are the "visuo-spatial sketch pad," which handles visual images and the "phonological loop," dedicated to speech sounds. The phonological loop model is especially important for language processing.

The phonological loop might be thought of as a loop of recording tape. Only speech sounds can be recorded on this loop. The loop acts as a buffer space to temporarily store incoming speech information. Remember that the process of recognizing words and sentences is thought to involve many comparisons of heard information with stored information at various levels of analysis. Further, understanding sentences requires computation of the relationships between words based on their grammatical markers and their positions in the sentence. When we know a lot about language, much of what we hear can be understood easily without referring to what might be recorded on this loop and the information on it is quickly erased as it is replaced by a new message.

However, the phonological loop provides us access to the sequence of phonemes (speech sounds) we just heard. It serves as a fallback we can refer to if what we hear does not immediately make sense or if there are words we don't understand. Recent research by Baddeley and his colleagues has determined that the main function of the phonological loop is for learning vocabulary and grammatical structures. But it also serves to hold sentences long enough to do whatever grammatical computations are required for comprehension. This ability to hold on to sounds for a brief period also allows us to use context to solve ambiguities in sentences and to guess about words we did not hear clearly.

Unfortunately, the phonological loop and, thus working memory capacity, is limited. This puts some limits on comprehension and learning. Interestingly, Baddeley's experiments have shown that it is not the number of items that can be stored that is limited. The phonological loop is limited in time. The loop seems to be of about 1.5 to 2 seconds duration. Thus our memory span consists of the number of items that can be produced in 1.5 to 2 seconds.

We must remember that Baddeley's model acknowledges that simultaneous use of the phonological loop for another task may interfere with learning, but does not prevent learning entirely. Thus, problems with the phonological loop may interfere with comprehension or learning, but do not completely prevent these activities from taking place. Baddeley's phonological loop model gives a good picture of how working memory may be handling speech information. However, it is only a model. Other researchers, such as Just and Carpenter, have different models of working memory which do not include the phonological loop. Their model depends on the total amount of resource (they call it activation) available to working memory to support both storage and processing.

So, in both adults and children, memory span puts limits on the capacity and thus, the effectiveness, of working memory during language processing. If the amount of information that can be held in working memory is too limited, long sentences might be misunderstood. Or some new words and sentence structures may not be learned well enough to become automatic. Likewise, if one link in the processing chain, say, word recognition or grammatical computation, is carried out too slowly it can cause a bottleneck in the flow of incoming information. When this happens information is lost from the working memory buffer before it can be analyzed. It is forgotten before it is understood. A backlog of new information is not the only thing which can clog the working memory buffer. Interference from multiple messages can also cause problems. And even worries, preoccupations and our own thoughts seem to be able to use up working memory capacity and interfere with information processing.

Bottom-up and top-down processing

The burgeoning field of neuroscience has produced many exciting results. We are gaining a better and better understanding of how our brains do all the amazing things they do, including processing language. Although we do not yet know exactly what pattern of neuron firing is responsible for which bit of information, we do understand something about the kinds of processes we need to manage language information effectively. Experiments have shown that we use both bottom-up and top-down processes.

Bottom-up processes work on sensory input. As described in the previous chapter, incoming auditory information is segmented (broken into separate words), coded, and matched to previously stored knowledge about words. When enough sensory information is received and analyzed the listener will recognize a familiar word. As more words are recognized the meaning of the message begins to become apparent. Unfortunately, many factors such as environmental noise and other intrusions combine to interfere with the clarity of the messages reaching our ears. Our brain's solution to this chronic problem is to use top-down processing.

Top-down processes work to understand the meaning by using information about the context of the message. Context can be understood at a number of levels. At the environmental level, knowing who is speaking, the place of the conversation and other details about the situation provide useful information about what is being said. At a different level, the previous sentences and the other words in a sentence establish a semantic (meaning) context. Knowing what the sentence is about helps in guessing about the meaning of a new or obscured word. Knowledge of word ordering and sound system rules also allow a listener to make top-down decisions based on these systems. Bottom-up and top-down processing work simultaneously and additively to come up with the best guess about a message.

In order to understand the importance of context, let's return to the analogy of "Name that Tune". A single note does not give us enough information to recognize a song. If the melody is hummed or picked out on a piano, we might recognize the tune after a handful of notes. But, as the game is often played, the first note of a popular recording of a song is provided. Here there is often a great deal of contextual information to help. The melody note may be in the context of simultaneous harmony notes. And, the first note or two can include important clues about the instrumentation or vocal quality of the piece and thus may reveal something about type of music, the musical group, composer or artist. It is this extra contextual information which gives us the clues necessary to guess the tune after only 1 or 2 notes. So it is with understanding of speech. By bringing every bit of pertinent information to bear, we can interpret messages very effectively.

At this point an example might help to make things a bit clearer. A recent experience brought the importance of contextual clues home to me. At 7:45 one Tuesday morning I was in the kitchen of our two-story home when my husband called down to me from upstairs. I could hear that he was saying something but I could not make out a single word of the message. But within a few seconds I knew what he had said. How did I figure it out? I based my correct guess on a number of clues in an almost exclusively top-down analysis. I could tell that the utterance was a question because it ended with rising intonation. I knew how many syllables long the question was but not how many words were in it and I perceived the general rhythmic and melodic shape of the sentence. I could tell by the fact that he called from a distance that this was a matter that needed to be addressed, but his tone of voice did not indicate extreme urgency. I was aware that it was Tuesday. All these clues came together after a few seconds and I realized that he had asked "Did you take out the garbage?" This example struck me because I realized that I was processing the sentence so slowly that I could "see" how it was happening. With almost no speech sound information but only the the length, rhythm and intonation of the sentence to guide me I was slow to understand. But with lots of help from context, I did, in fact, interpret the sentence correctly.

This was an unusual case. The auditory information was muffled and indistinct because of the distance. Neither could I get any visual information about what sounds were being produced because my partner was out of sight. I had to depend on what I knew about the situation, the structure of the language, and about my husband, who seldom takes out the garbage, but has a good memory.

There are other situations when we have to depend mainly on bottom-up processing. This happens when we don't have enough contextual information. When making a new acquaintance one of the first things we usually learn is the person's name. If our new friend's name is Fred Smith or Sue Johnson we normally don't have any trouble understanding it. We are quite familiar with the sounds that make up these names and have had previous experience with the names Fred, Sue, Smith and Johnson. To be sure, the fact that these names are easy to process and understand does not imply that they will be particularly easy to remember. But, that is a different problem.

Now, what if you meet Nopparat Kaewphakdee or Uwe Nurmesniemi. Unless you speak Thai or Finnish your experience probably does not provide you with familiar models to match these names. You will be entirely dependent on what you hear in trying to reconstruct the appropriate sound sequence. You may not even be familiar with the sounds and sound combinations that occur in these languages. Thus, trying to remember the sequence of sounds in both first and last names is likely to overload your working memory capacity. You may have to be content with correctly producing only Nop or Mr. Nur.

In such a circumstance most people need to hear the new name several times before they can learn it. Others find it necessary to see the name in writing before they can remember it. Writing allows us to put sounds on paper where they can't escape. That way we are not overwhelmed by trying to remember the unfamiliar sound sequence and we can slow down the process of analyzing and committing the new name to memory. When words are written, visual memory can share the burden of learning them.

4

MODES OF LANGUAGE PROCESSING

Now we understand some of the processes that take place during the perception and comprehension of spoken language. But being a proficient language user means more than just being able to understand the speech of others. We also express ourselves. We usually do that by speaking, but sometimes we use visual rather than vocal means to communicate with others. In this chapter we explore the role of language processing in various ways or modes of communication.

Input processing and output processing

In previous chapters we have focused on the processing of verbal input—understanding what we hear. What about speaking? While a linguistic message is being analyzed top-down and bottom-up, a best guess at the ideas encoded in the message is being computed. Successful analysis and computation results in comprehension. A response is already beginning to take shape as comprehension takes place.

A spoken response entails output processing. Output processing is even more complicated than input processing. It involves putting your thoughts and ideas into words, ordering the words and directing the speech muscles to produce an utterance. The pattern of sound waves thus created carries the message you are trying to express to your listener.

Output processing is the chain of events that takes place through our brains and nerves during the formulation and production of speech. It includes locating the correct sound sequences that make up the words we want to express. If you have ever found yourself groping for a word you know that you know, you will agree that it is usually more difficult to locate the specific sound sequence that names a concept than to connect meaning with a word you hear. In addition to finding the words needed to respond, the order of the words must be planned and the forms of verbs, pronouns and nouns must be brought into agreement with each other and with grammatical rules. All this takes place within the context of working memory.

Programs that direct muscles to produce the speech sounds of the sentence in the correct order must also be engaged. These plans will include instructions for the stress, intonation and rhythm of the sentence. This work goes on quite automatically most of the time, but we do sometimes become aware of weak points in output processing. Even eloquent speakers occasionally have trouble finding a word, make subtle grammatical errors, experience slips of the tongue or reverse words (remember Reverend Spooner).

Auditory and visual language processing

So far, our descriptions of language processing have referred mainly to the processing of spoken language. But language processing problems are not limited to spoken language. In our daily life we are often called upon to understand and use written language. Unfortunately, writing language down adds a layer of code to the puzzle. After all, letters are just squiggles on paper which stand for speech sounds. This additional processing level makes written language harder to use than speech.

Reading is a human ability which is derived from our spoken language ability. Because it is based on speech, the use of written language came along after spoken language and its development took considerable time. In addition, for much of recorded history the scribes, who learned to read and write, represented a very small fraction of any population. It has only been in the past few hundred years that ordinary people have been reading and writing. Therefore these abilities are not as strongly supported by our neural wiring as listening and speaking are. This is why reading and writing are more difficult for children to learn than listening and speaking.

On the other hand, there are obvious advantages in being able to write things down and read them later. Written language endures. We can look at it over and over again. We often think of reading as a visual skill, but it is really a visually-mediated language skill. Learning to read depends crucially on a familiarity with spoken language. Learning to read is an important part of every child's education, but it is particularly helpful for children whose visual processing abilities are much stronger than their auditory processing abilities. In later chapters I will address the relationship between language processing problems and reading problems.

There are two other topics that should be mentioned in connection with visual processing of language; sign language and lipreading. They are both ways that meaning can be transferred by visual rather than auditory signals. Each deserves a book of its own and they will not be treated in detail since the main focus of this book is on spoken language processing. However, both of them have been used successfully with children to augment auditory language processing.

American Sign Language (ASL) and other forms of sign language are complete systems of language which depend wholly on visual processing for comprehension. Deaf people are able to communicate all their thoughts and ideas through these visually-based systems. Sign language is used, quite successfully, to stimulate spoken language development in young children with delays in beginning to speak. Seeing the sign and learning to make it provide visual and tactile representations which can help these children learn and remember the spoken form of a word.

Lip-reading is another way language can be processed visually. Even for a listener with good hearing, watching a speaker's mouth provides many useful clues to deciphering what sounds are being produced. Many adult listeners and some children use these clues automatically, (that is, without realizing they are doing so) to aid in language processing. However, many children who could benefit do not make use of this kind of visual information.

5

HOW DO CHILDREN LEARN TO PROCESS LANGUAGE?

Learning language is a puzzle posed to each new human being. Making sense out of spoken utterances is complicated. How does an infant break the code and get started using language? Many other books describe what we know about the amazing feat of learning language. For our purposes it is most important to know that from the moment of birth (and even before) the child is working on the problem. During the period of prenatal development and in early infancy the human brain experiences an explosion of development. Billions of brain cells form and connect with each other. Some of these connections enable the infant to perceive and differentiate a vast array of speech sounds. Thus the child is ready to learn any language on earth. However during the first six months of life most of the connections for sounds not used in the child's own language environment degenerate from disuse. It is this very process of pruning or clearing away unnecessary connections which allows the child to focus on the important sound distinctions of his own language. This same kind of process is involved in learning at every level. Thus the total number of neural connections is continually being reduced through the years of growth and development and throughout life.

Learning the sound system of your native language happens so early in life that you normally don't remember anything about the learning process. But you developed an inventory of the sounds used in your language and the ability to divide the speech stream into words. The clues we use to break a stream of sound into words are so subtle that we are almost completely unaware of them. We attend to things like stress, rhythm and syllabification to do it.

Apparently, speakers of different languages use different clues to separate the sound stream into words. So recognizing unique patterns of stress and rhythm is one of the first things we learn about our language and doing so permanently marks us as native speakers of that language. A child can usually learn to use another system to segment a sound stream into words and thus can learn to speak other languages without an accent. But if, as a child, you have only ever used one language, then in adulthood it becomes much harder (or impossible) to change the way you use stress, rhythm and syllabification. This is the basis of recognizable accents in people who have changed languages in adulthood.

In addition to listening from birth to the language around her, the infant soon begins practicing with her vocal instrument, experimenting with various ways of making sounds. After about one year of working on the language puzzle, the average child begins to use a few words. First attempts at ordering words in simple two-word sentences typically come between the first and second birthdays.

We know that in our daily use of language, knowledge and processing are interdependent and must work together. But, which comes first when learning language? Understanding a sentence depends on knowing the words in it. But learning new words depends on understanding (being able to process) the sentence in which they are heard. So processing depends on knowledge and knowledge depends on processing. In order to learn language the beginner must figuratively grab onto whatever handhold she can. Then alternately making small gains in processing and knowledge she can pull herself up by the bootstraps to more and more effective language use.

During the course of language development the bootstrapping continues. While learning new vocabulary words and the rules of grammar, the child must practice using language so that the data

and rules can be accessed rapidly and automatically. This automa-
tization is essential for normal communicative interactions. This
rapid, automatic processing of language, both bottom-up and top-
down, is called on-line processing because it takes place on-line,
that is, it happens at the same time the child is engaged in communicating. On-line processing has to happen automatically because during communication, the child's attention is engaged by
the information being transmitted. There is rarely time for catch-
up or reflection. It is this on-line language processing that is addressed in the remainder of the book.

6

PROBLEMS WITH LANGUAGE PROCESSING

Defining the problem

Now that we have a basic understanding of how language is processed we will explore the kinds of problems that can be associated with this amazing ability. The problems may be mild to severe, simple to complex and temporary, intermittent or long term. On-line language processing has the advantages of being rapid and automatic. But the disadvantage is that its complexity and the circumstances of its use make it quite vulnerable to interference.

The fact that we sometimes have processing problems is not surprising. Information bombards our senses and our brains are continuously perceiving and processing this sensory information. This processing allows us to experience recognizable images, odors, tastes and sounds. Spoken language makes up a part of the sensory information we receive every day and it is a fantastically complicated system. As we learned in Chapter 2, language is a layered set of systems including sound, grammar and meaning. Understanding language requires us to simultaneously decode all the layers. This complexity means that the processing of spoken language is prone to breakdowns. Try to imagine yourself in the following situations. These examples demonstrate language processing difficulties which can happen to anyone.

Interfering noise or message. The person sitting next to you coughs over the most important line in the movie. Or, you are talking on the phone and someone comes into the room and begins a conversation. You can hear both speakers but you probably can't understand either one.

Message too long, too complex or too disorganized. You ask directions and are told a long list of streets, stop lights and right and left turns. Unless you are very familiar with the neighborhood you are confused after the first few instructions.

Message too fast. Oldsters often have this kind of trouble understanding teens. And what about the rush-hour traffic report? If you are not ready to hear the specific information you need, forget it.

Unfamiliar vocabulary. Remember that lecture in astrophysics you attended by accident? You understand English, but the vocabulary sounds like Greek to you. Processing so many new words at one time can overwhelm your working memory capacity.

Unfamiliar accent. Even though English speakers should be mutually intelligible, we sometimes meet speakers from other parts of the United States or the world who sound so different to us that we have trouble understanding them. When we have to slow down or back up to make sense of unfamiliar sound patterns our on-line processing can fall behind and we lose part of the message.

Foreign country. This one brings several of the above factors together in an example that really makes it clear how it feels to have a severe language processing problem. Did you study Spanish or French or German in school? Maybe you have traveled to a country where the language you studied was spoken. You know the language well enough to ask a basic question about where to find something you need. But then comes the answer. You probably found that you did not understand much of what was said. Unfamiliar vocabulary, unfamiliar accent, message too long and too fast and very little knowledge about the local environment to help. Wham!

Now that we have an idea how it feels to have a language processing problem, let's find out more about how and why many children have such problems in their native language.

Some impediments to using spoken language are easy to understand. Deafness interferes with reception of sound information. If the speech signal cannot be heard, the brain cannot process the auditory information. There are also some obvious problems with speech production. In some forms of cerebral palsy the speech muscles cannot be well controlled. Language processing may take place normally for comprehension and even for planning a response, but the speech muscles will not follow the brain's instructions. Deafness and cerebral palsy are both caused by problems with nerve cells. These neurological defects result in obvious physiological roadblocks to the understanding or production of spoken language.

But, the effects of neurological defects or damage are not always so apparent. Within our brains, billions of nerve cells interconnect at many levels. Minor differences in the functioning or connection patterns of these neurons can have substantial effects on the ability to process language. Unfortunately, subtle deviations in neural structure and organization are often difficult or impossible to see. Modern imaging technology like computerized tomography (CT scans) and Magnetic Resonance Imaging (MRI) provide good quality pictures of the brain's structure. However, imaging technology is not yet precise enough to visualize some types of neurological abnormalities or differences. Maybe the deviations are too small to be observed. Or perhaps even the specialists don't know exactly what to look for. In particular, it may be the brain's behavior—the patterns of nerve activation—that are causing the difficulties. But since there is often little or no physical evidence of neurological damage in children with language processing problems, some professionals are skeptical of the diagnosis.

There is a further reason for skepticism among some educators. Problems with language processing can be so mild that they do not interfere much at all with communication or learning. As we just learned, it is quite normal to be faced with language processing problems under certain circumstances. You have experienced language processing problems if you have ever had difficulty understanding a spoken message. In addition to the problematic situations listed above, there are factors within ourselves which can interfere with processing. Being tired, ill, worried, distracted or self-conscious can slow down the rate of language processing or fill up working memory with extraneous verbal information. Language processing capacity is reduced in these situations, but this inefficiency is only temporary. Many educators ask "If language processing difficulties are so common and transitory, why should some children be given special consideration?"

On the other hand language processing problems can be very severe. This happens when there is significant damage to the brain or if the nervous system fails to develop normally. Sometimes the processing problems are so grave that they significantly delay or prevent language development. When this happens both language knowledge and processing are usually affected. Such severe language disorders are not usually labeled as language processing disorders because their effects are more broadly felt. Children with head injury, epilepsy, autism and many other neurological diagnoses exhibit various levels of language processing disturbance.

The processing problems which most concern us in this book fall between the extremes of mild, transient problems and severe language disorders. In particular, this book is addressed to the families and teachers of children who experience chronic language processing problems in spite of otherwise normal development. These children exhibit normal, and sometimes superior, knowledge of vocabulary and grammatical rules. There are many children who fall into this category. Some are clearly having problems in school or in social interactions. Others are managing to keep up by working very hard. Some succeed by making use of as many environmental cues as possible to compensate for their difficulties. But, most of them feel they are stupid in spite of the fact that they have average, above average or even superior intelligence.

These children vary, of course. Each exhibits a unique pattern of intellectual abilities. They vary in their individual strengths and weaknesses. They have different degrees and types of language processing problems. And they have different personalities and interests. But they share a consistent tendency to experience difficulty when processing language information. This compromises their ability to understand language, to express themselves using language, or both. Of most concern are the children who have language processing problems without more obvious symptoms of language disability. Because these children are not usually identified by routine language testing, they are typically not offered any kind of assistance in school, despite the difficulties they may be having. And these same children are often the target of criticism and jokes at school, at home and among peers.

Fortunately some educators are becoming more aware of the effects of language processing problems. But all too often teachers describe these children as inattentive, lazy, stubborn, confused or worse. The children themselves often are frustrated with their situation and may have low self-esteem. Depending on the child's personality and his environment these feelings can lead to withdrawal, clowning or aggressive behavior.

Often, however, children's language processing problems are recognized by their parents. The following are the most common complaints parents make about these children:

Can't follow directions; doesn't pay attention; doesn't listen.

Frequently needs repetition to understand; often says "huh?" or "what?"

Can't remember what he was told from one day (or minute) to the next.

Has trouble thinking of words; uses general terms like "thing" or "guy" rather than more specific names for items or people.

Has trouble expressing herself; restarts and revises sentences many times.

Seems confused, reticent or disoriented, especially in new situations.

Often teachers report similar problems. Many teachers are aware of children's language processing problems. They may observe a child who is overwhelmed by the noise level and the competing messages generated in the classroom. Another child may perform best on assignments which involve working individually, but have difficulty when classes are taught by lecture and learning depends primarily on listening.

Both parents and teachers are often perplexed by the problems they see in children with language processing problems. These children do not all have the same kinds of difficulties. And even more puzzling, a child's performance may fluctuate from day to day. Although there appears to be no reason for the fluctuation, subtle changes in the situation can make the difference. These may include changes in the child or in the materials. Being tired, hungry, upset or distracted may compound a child's processing problems and compromise her memory. But a change in the format or context of the subject matter from one day to another is just as likely to cause problems. For these reasons it is usually difficult to pin down the problem and put a label on it.

What causes language processing problems?

Problems can occur at any point in the processing of language input or output. Because processing is a chain of events, the effects of a small problem early in the chain can accumulate, causing a significant detriment to overall language processing. Problems can be broad or specific and have effects which are mild to severe. And they can vary depending upon what other demands are being placed on the system.

Some children mainly have trouble processing language input, while others have difficulty with output processing. For still others there are problems with both. It is usually not possible to say exactly what is causing a child's processing problems. But the problems which I encounter most frequently appear to result from difficulties in a few specific areas.

Input processing problems seem to result from difficulties with speech sound perception and/or working memory. Inefficient speech perception can result in errors or indecision about the incoming information. Even subtle speech perception difficulties may cause such a slowdown in language processing that it becomes impossible to hold on to speech sound information long enough to decode it. This effect serves to reduce (essentially waste) working memory span. Another obstacle to input processing is competition for working memory resources. If a child can not screen out extraneous verbal information from the environment or from his own inner thoughts these irrelevant words might use up working memory capacity and interfere with processing of language input.

Children with output processing problems often have trouble finding the sound sequences that represent the ideas they want to express. Such word-retrieval problems are experienced by all of us, but for some children the problem occurs much too frequently. Other children may not have trouble retrieving words, but cannot efficiently organize their thoughts into sentences. This problem may reflect limited working memory capacity. Or the child may have insufficient knowledge of the grammatical mechanisms for forming sentences and defining relationships between ideas in a sentence. Even if he knows enough about grammar to organize a sentence properly, the child may not be able to use this information automatically enough to keep up in a conversation. Failing to learn how to use these grammatical mechanisms may, in turn, be due to limited ability to remember the sentences which contain them. Over and above these problems with word retrieval and sentence formulation, some children have difficulty ordering sentences to tell a coherent story.

Understanding these proximate causes of language processing problems is helpful. However, it does not tell us the ultimate cause of a child's processing difficulty. Why does Jason have limited working memory span? What makes Jessica have poor speech perception? Unfortunately it is usually impossible to answer these questions with certainty. But often we can point to one or more factors which could be involved. These may include medical or environmental factors such as birth difficulties, neurological conditions, ear disease, trauma, etc., and/or genetic factors such as a family history of speech, language or reading problems. In the following chapters we will try to sort through a variety of terms and definitions relating to language processing problems and see how language processing problems relate to other language and learning problems.

7

CONFUSIONS OF TERMINOLOGY

What's in a name?

"Language processing" is the way I describe the chain of sensory and neurological events which results in our understanding of verbal information and our ability to formulate a verbal response. There are other terms which have been used interchangeably to describe this process. You may have heard terms such as "auditory processing problem" or "central auditory processing disorder". The problems described have also been dubbed "auditory comprehension deficit", and in the past "word deafness" or "central deafness". There continues to be some disagreement among practitioners about the best name for the problem. To some degree there is also confusion about what abilities make up language processing.

I have chosen to use the term "language processing". In comparison, "auditory processing", and "central auditory processing," can imply processing of all kinds of auditory information whether linguistic or nonlinguistic. It certainly is important to be able to recognize the nature and direction of environmental sounds (e.g., a car approaching from behind or a pot boiling over in the kitchen). However, being able to do this does not preclude having difficulty processing language.

There are test batteries available to diagnose central auditory processing disorders (CAPD). These tests typically evaluate the ability to understand speech in noise, to sort out competing messages, to recognize tone patterns, etc. They are administered and interpreted by audiologists. If your child is having processing problems it would be worthwhile to find our whether her problems have a central auditory basis. However, many children who are clearly having problems processing language do not have CAPD. Conversely, almost all children with CAPD exhibit difficulty processing language.

I also reject the use of "auditory comprehension deficit" as a description of language processing problems. "Auditory comprehension deficit" is validly used to describe difficulties understanding language, but it is a more general term which traditionally does not distinguish between "language knowledge" and "language processing". Further, all these terms focus on "auditory" information, implying a focus on spoken language input. The term "language processing" applies both to understanding language and to formulating language output. In addition "language processing" does not specify that the input or output be "auditory". Thus the term can include reading and written language as well. Throughout this book the term language processing refers to on-line processing. On-line processing takes place during language use, whether listening, speaking, reading or writing.

Severity

There is also confusion about how to indicate the severity of language processing problems. Is this a disorder, deficit, difficulty, disability, impairment, problem or just a concern? As with many conditions, some of the symptoms of language processing problems are experienced by everyone.

As we saw in Chapter 6, each of us experiences minor misunderstandings during verbal interactions every day. These are normal and expected due to the nature of language and are usually easily resolved. Moreover, we have all been in more unusual situations when we found understanding or making ourselves understood much more difficult than usual because of physical or emotional stress. We also know that on the opposite end of the continuum there are children (and adults) whose ability to process language is severely impaired. However there is a broad range of language processing ability between these two extremes. There are many children experiencing speech, language, learning or reading problems. Many of those children are receiving speech-language therapy or special help with language or reading skills. Some of them are receiving treatment which focuses on developing strategies for improved language processing, but for the majority treatment addresses mainly language knowledge. And many children, especially those whose problems are with language processing rather than language knowledge, are judged not to have severe enough difficulties to warrant special services. Thus, a considerable number of children are struggling, unaided, with language-based instruction and social interactions.

Keeping in mind that language processing problems are a component of most language disorders, in this book I use the term "language processing problem" (from hereon, LPP) in a special sense. I am usually referring to those children whose problems in this domain are greater or more persistent than those experienced by "normal" language users but who are not identified as language impaired by the typical tests used to measure language ability. To what degree the impairment of function is perceived as a concern, problem or disability will depend on the individual circumstances.

8

INTRINSIC FACTORS
RELATED TO LPP

There are a number of areas of confusion and overlap between language processing problems and other traits or conditions. In this chapter we will explore the relationships between LPP and certain factors which are intrinsic, that is, come from within the child. Intrinsic factors include genetic and neurological predispositions or conditions. For example, questions about intelligence and attention deficit disorder come up in almost every conversation I have with parents about language processing problems. Although the various topics discussed below may seem unrelated they all have important connections with LPP.

Intelligence

There is constant, ongoing debate about the nature of intelligence and whether it can be validly tested. In spite of the debate most schools continue to use some measure of intelligence quotient (IQ) to predict students' school performance. Whether their comments are based on IQ scores or on other observations, parents and teachers frequently make statements like "I don't understand why Judy is having so much trouble in school. She seems so intelligent". The interaction between language processing problems and intelligence is complex. Many IQ tests are heavily language dependent. There is a strong and well-known correlation between IQ and vocabulary knowledge. Thus, if vocabulary knowledge is the main focus of an IQ test, a child with a mild language processing problem may do very well. But most IQ tests used with children include verbal instructions and many depend on verbal responses. When tests draw more on language processing than on language knowledge, many children with LPP can be expected to have some difficulty and thus score lower than they would on a test of vocabulary knowledge.

There is no simple connection between language processing abilities and performance on various IQ subtests. Different children have trouble with different aspects of language processing. And the language processing demands of subtests vary considerably. For example, a "Vocabulary" test that measures recognition of words is much less demanding than one that requires a child to define words. The former usually requires a child to point to one picture out of several that best depicts a word spoken by the examiner. This does not usually put the child with LPP at a disadvantage. Defining a word, however, requires much more language processing and LPP children usually have more trouble with it. And it might seem that scores on "Computation" measures would not be much affected by language processing difficulties. But these scores can be unrepresentative of a child's true mathematical ability if the task is to solve word problems. In other words, the format of the test can be more important than the subject in determining the LPP child's performance.

A considerable amount of research has been carried out with the aim of shedding light on the relationship between language (knowledge and processing) and intelligence. Results of these studies show two very different trends. On the one hand, a person's performance on various measures of intelligence tends to cluster around a certain level. But equally important research has resulted in the notion of a number of separate intelligences that can be at quite different levels. In my clinical experience I have seen a wide range of IQ scores in children with LPP. In fact many children with LPP exhibit noticeable variance in their performance on separate subtests in a single IQ test. The effect is less noticeable when the subtest scores are averaged together. But it is very apparent when subtests which rely heavily on language processing are singled out. Some of the highest scores I have ever seen on nonverbal measures such as copying complex block designs were achieved by children with significant language processing problems.

Could this be because these children have exercised their visual/spatial skills in attempting to compensate for their language processing difficulties? There is no doubt that children naturally try to compensate for their difficulties by using other abilities. They sometimes develop problem-solving strategies that are specifically designed to help them process language more effectively. Children with higher overall intelligence may be more successful at doing this. However personality and temperament must also be involved. Some children are so successful at using alternative strategies that their impairments may not be apparent even to those closest to them.

Attention Deficit Disorder

Language processing does depend on being able to attend to language information. Children with language processing problems often exhibit symptoms such as difficulty following directions, frequent requests for repetition, daydreaming, or being "lost". Thus they are frequently thought to be inattentive and are diagnosed with attention deficit disorder (ADD). ADD is probably the most popular diagnosis for school-age children these days. But this diagnosis is often arrived at too hastily. Some children do have trouble understanding because they are not paying attention, but with LPP children the direction of causality is reversed. They are not attending because they don't understand. The best way to differentiate between a child with ADD and one with LPP is to observe them in language and non-language activities. A child may be fidgety and inattentive during language-based activities such as class discussion, story time and even many TV shows. But with a switch to non-language activities such as puzzles, art projects or active play the LPP child no longer has any difficulty attending appropriately to the task. The child with ADD would have equal difficulty attending to both types of activities.

Language Learning Disability and Specific Language Impairment

In order to attend to language-based activities at his age level, a child must be able to process language efficiently. And processing efficiency depends to some degree on language knowledge. Language Learning Disability (LLD) and Specific Language Impairment (SLI) involve difficulty with both language knowledge and language processing. They both tend to run in families and are thus probably genetically based. The two terms may refer to the same disorder.

Children with LPP are sometimes identified as having a language learning disability (LLD). And that diagnosis is justified if the processing difficulties are pronounced, especially if the child is having other problems with language such as limited vocabulary or grammatical skills. Children with this diagnosis usually receive remedial services in school, although the treatment offered may not target language processing specifically.

Specific language impairment (SLI) is another diagnosis which is typically used for children with language problems. There is some disagreement about this category. In general, the term refers to a disorder which is specific to language skills. Children with SLI, by definition do not exhibit a general learning disability or a general intellectual deficit. But, they score below the average range of performance for their age on one or more measures of language ability. Because most available language tests do not separate language knowledge from language processing ability, it is impossible to know for sure which is the main problem. However, because a child's language performance must be significantly impaired to qualify for the diagnosis of SLI, most children diagnosed with SLI have difficulty with both language knowledge and processing.

Unfortunately we do not yet have enough data to fully understand specific language impairment and language learning disabilities. Whatever the specific cause of their problems, these children do learn language. But they have a tendency to exhibit specific difficulties. They usually need to hear new words more times than normal children before learning them. They have difficulty learning to use grammatical structures and this difficulty extends to their ability to imitate sentences containing these structures. In particular they have trouble learning to use correct forms of pronouns and to correctly construct verb forms. They also have trouble restating an idea in other words. This deficiency makes it hard for SLI and LLD children to clarify their meaning when they are not understood. Unfortunately, many children with these language disorders will continue to struggle with certain aspects of language for years.

At this point I think it is important to clarify a point about language disorders and language processing problems. In general most children with receptive language disorders (problems understanding) or expressive language disorders (problems expressing themselves) or a combination of the two do also have problems processing language (input, output or both). In this book I have defined a separate population of children, with LPP, who have problems processing language input, output or both but who usually attain average scores on typical language tests, especially those mainly measuring language knowledge.

It turns out that there are also some children who exhibit normal language processing abilities but who show deficits in language knowledge. This can be the case for children from ethnic, cultural or economic backgrounds which differ from the norm of society. If a child's experiences are such that he is unfamiliar with the vocabulary, sentence structure or the test format used in typical language tests then he may perform below average when judged by the test norms. Recent studies by Chris Dollaghan and Tho-

mas Campbell and their associates tested children using both knowledge-dependent and processing-dependent measures. The processing-dependent tests were designed to minimize the contribution
of prior language knowledge. They found no difference in performance between children from minority groups and those in the
majority on the processing-dependent tests. This was so in spite of
the fact that minority children in the studies scored significantly
lower on the knowledge-dependent language tests.

Auditory temporal processing deficit

Paula Tallal and her colleagues have carried out long-term research on children with developmental language impairments. They
have been particularly interested in these children's ability to process the basic sound features of language. Their research has revealed that some people cannot perceive sensory signals of very
short duration. Why might this deficit affect speech comprehension? Because speech sounds take place over time. The sound seg-
ments which represent vowels typically last for as long as 250 msec.
However, consonants are distinguished from one another by very
rapid changes of frequency. The parts of the speech signal which
characterize certain consonant sounds are less than 50 msec in
duration. The frequency transition which differentiates /b/ from
/d/, for example, happens so fast that some people do not perceive
it. Difficulty perceiving rapid sound transitions results in a problem identifying and categorizing the basic sounds of language. It
is a language processing problem at the phonological level. This
type of disorder seems to occur in at least some of the population
with LLD and SLI.

Whether a phonological processing deficit can be severe enough
in itself to cause a language impairment or whether other factors
are involved, children with phonological processing deficits do have
trouble learning language. Their difficulty recognizing the distinctions between some sounds can interfere with comprehension.
Confusion in categorizing phonemes also may lead some children

to exhibit errors when they produce speech sounds. For children with language disorders there is probably a complex interaction going on between auditory perception, phonological awareness, speech production, memory span and language learning, and the effects most likely vary considerably among children.

Phonological processing problem

It is quite possible that phonological processing difficulties could also be at the root of language processing problems less severe than SLI or LLD. You might think that being unable to distinguish between some consonant sounds would cause extreme confusion. But, much of the time the problem is not even noticed. A person with mild phonological processing difficulties might confuse the words "big" and "dig" if she heard them in isolation. But we normally hear words in context. Context provides information about the probable meaning and function of words. Even if there was no clue to the first consonant, normal language users would know which was which by the context. We wouldn't expect someone to ask for "the dig cookie" or to "big in the sand". Thus context usually leads to the correct interpretation when phonological information is missing.

Once we have learned language, we forget how much we depend on context. Adults with mild phonological processing problems still tend to have difficulty when certain sounds occur in unfamiliar words. This is especially true when contextual information is limited. If you hear an unfamiliar name during a radio broadcast can you tell if it is Bailey or Daly? If you can't, you might have a phonological processing problem. Like any language processing problem, the degree to which it interferes with your life depends on its severity and the compensatory strategies, both conscious and unconscious, you are able to use to get around it.

Contextual information does automatically fill in gaps in phonological information. The system works fine when there is not much to process. But there is a cost for this convenience. As we listen to speech we briefly hold some of the incoming sound information in working memory. When we listen to someone talking at length we are using working memory as a buffer to hold onto information long enough to sort out the ambiguities and make sense of it. We do this constantly as we listen to a teacher lecturing, the news report, movie dialogue or a friend telling about her vacation.

The trouble is that phonological processing difficulties mean backtracking. In order to resolve the first sound of the first word spoken it might be necessary to have information from the end of the sentence. This means that more processing time and capacity are needed. Since new information is constantly arriving, working memory can't always keep up. This causes a bottleneck of information which interferes with comprehension. The result is that you end up missing part of the message.

Difficulties perceiving phonological distinctions, in addition to causing working memory congestion, can also lead to problems with long-term storage of phonological information. New words may be stored incorrectly or a word may be stored in two different ways on two different occasions. Having inconsistent or competing versions of a word then leads to inefficient word retrieval. Problems storing or retrieving the sound sequences of words may cause various language problems, including LPP.

Other neurological impairments

Although the above topics cover many of the areas related to LPP, the list is by no means exhaustive. There is a wide range of neurological conditions, which, even in their mildest form, result in LPP. Some of these conditions result from trauma occurring before, during or after birth, and some are the result of genetic conditions. They include cerebral palsy, hydrocephalus, epilepsy, neurofibromatosis, head injury, Tourette's syndrome, just to name a few. However, because language processing is such a complex activity, it can be disrupted even by very mild neurological differences and ones that are not nearly as obvious, recognizable and nameable as the examples just given.

Dyslexia

There are many misconceptions about dyslexia. It is yet another neurological condition. This one affects the specific skill of reading. Dyslexia means difficulty with reading or inability to learn to read. Many children struggle with reading, but when a school-age child's reading skills are far poorer than his oral language skills or overall intelligence would predict, a disorder specific to reading is suspected.

Dyslexia or specific reading problem is a processing problem. The processing difficulty occurs in translating between the auditory and visual representations of language. This does not mean that dyslexia is a visual problem. To the contrary, it is a language-based problem. It is a specific difficulty using the alphabetic coding system that "names" certain sounds as "letters". For most of us the levels of processing involved in reading are inaccessible because we long ago learned to read automatically. But for the child learning to read the complexity may be formidable. The processing problems of dyslexia are often accompanied by difficulties processing spoken language.

It has long been known that dyslexia runs in families. Through family genetic studies, researchers have recently found the locations of several genes which are thought to put children at risk of dyslexia. There is some further evidence that language processing problems without dyslexia run in these same families.

In this chapter we found that LPP can be confused with and coexist with other neurological problems. We also saw that a tendency toward LPP (and other neurological conditions) is often transmitted genetically. And we learned that the expression (i.e., how an individual experiences the disorder) of LPP depends on the interplay of factors such as intelligence, speech sound discrimination and encoding ability.

9

EXTRINSIC FACTORS RELATED TO LPP

In addition to the genetic and neurological conditions which are associated with LPP, there are also extrinsic factors which relate to LPP. In other words there are effects that come from outside the child (from the environment) which can give rise to LPP. In this chapter we will address several of these extrinsic factors.

Sensory deprivation

Our brains learn to process information as we develop. Children who are deprived of sensory information as infants do not learn how to use it. If a child born blind or deaf is later given the ability to see or hear (perhaps through cataract surgery or a cochlear implant), she does not immediately know how to use these gifts. A normal infant's brain is working very hard during the first months and years to sort, categorize and interpret what it sees and hears. This learning takes time as well as appropriate sensory stimulation.

Recent studies indicate that the infant's brain is uniquely set up to solve the problem of making sense out of its environment. The developing brain establishes specific neural connections when exposed to normal sensory stimulation. These connections strengthen and elaborate through continued experience with sensory input. If sensory information is not available during early development, the brain's wiring becomes established anyway, but not in the specific way that is tuned to normal sensory input. It is much harder to make these connections later in childhood.

Deafness and blindness are absolute forms of sensory deprivation. But even children born with normal sight and hearing can miss out on sensory information for other reasons. Because we are mainly concerned about language processing let's focus on what happens when a child does not receive enough information about language.

Middle ear disease

One of the most common causes of interference with language information is middle ear disease. Ear infection, or otitis media, is rampant among toddlers and increasingly frequent in infants. Fortunately most children suffer only occasional bouts of otitis media. But some children have chronic ear infections. Their illness is frequent and the effects often last for several months or more.

The extent to which otitis media causes later language and learning problems is a hotly debated issue. But it is well known that when otitis media is present it often causes conductive hearing loss. This is a temporary hearing loss. Fluid or pus in the middle ear acts as a muffler. It keeps sounds from being transmitted clearly to the inner ear and on to the brain.

The conductive hearing loss of otitis media often fluctuates. It can be better or worse throughout the day or throughout the period of illness. Fluctuating conductive hearing loss can actually be present for weeks or months following a bout of otitis media. But does fluctuating hearing loss constitute sensory deprivation? Some authorities assert that the conductive hearing loss associated with otitis media is not severe enough or of long enough duration to cause permanent language problems.

Many studies have been carried out to try answer the question. The studies have used different populations of children. They have had different definitions of language problems and different methods for determining severity of otitis media. Not surprisingly they arrived at different conclusions.

But let us think about what we know. We know that from birth infants are evaluating the speech sounds they hear. We know that the infant's brain is forming neural connections to discriminate between the sounds in his language. We know that some speech sounds are very similar. We know that even a mild hearing loss can obscure the distinctions between similar sounds. We know that otitis media causes some degree of temporary hearing loss in many children. We know that in some children otitis media is chronic. We know that many of these children may have fluctuating hearing loss for months or years. We know that otitis media can occur in the earliest months of life.

A period of mild or fluctuating hearing loss wouldn't have much effect on you or me. Once you have learned a phonological system and developed the neural connections for using it, you don't forget it that easily. But what if you are trying to figure it out from scratch? A consistent, mild hearing loss would probably make it more difficult. But think about how hard it would be to learn the sounds of your language if the distinctions between speech sounds varied from day to day or week to week. In this situation an infant may not have enough clear and specific information to recognize the correct set of speech sounds of his language. Or he may develop more than one neural representation for a single phoneme. If the variation in input is too confusing, the infant may just give up trying to figure it out. At this point we are only speculating, but if it is true, the result would be an ineffectively wired phonological system. This ineffective system would most likely result in delays and bottlenecks and generally inefficient language processing.

Institutionalization

Sensory deprivation can also occur through neglect. The level of neglect required to interfere with language development is considerable. Most of the children I have seen with language processing problems arising from neglect have spent much of their infancy in institutions. Due to war or other dire situations, some countries of the world have many children without homes or families to care for them. Sometimes the orphanages which house these children do not have adequate staff to interact with them. In addition, children who have lost their homes and families have often suffered significant emotional trauma. A child who withdraws from social interaction or is consistently left alone and ignored is getting neither the language stimulation nor the emotional support to develop normally. Unless the situation is corrected fairly early this child runs the risk of significant problems processing language and regulating emotions and behavior.

Thus, there are a number of environmental conditions which seem to have the effect of producing language processing problems. To be sure these conditions do not produce the same effect all the time on all children. The individual propensities of each child are part of the total equation. Children differ in the strength of their inborn language abilities. Thus, some may need less input than others to succeed. One child might respond quite differently to desertion or neglect than another. It might also be claimed that some children have a genetic predisposition to suffering otitis media which, in turn, puts them at greater risk of language processing problems.

10

SUMMARIZING LANGUAGE PROCESSING PROBLEMS

No matter what the apparent cause of their problems, every one of the children I have encountered who fits the narrow definition of LPP has been different. Most of them have some difficulty following spoken commands. But some have more trouble understanding long sentences while others have more difficulty with grammatical complexity. Some LPP children show good comprehension of fairly long passages, but cannot repeat sentences accurately. Others can repeat quite well, but have difficulty with comprehension. I have also seen great variability in children's ability and willingness to use helpful strategies.

Children with LPP exhibit a wide range of other abilities. Some have strong abilities in visual analysis or visual memory to draw on. Strong interpretative or artistic skills can help compensate for language weaknesses. One child, who could not express himself easily in words drew intricate pictures to get his ideas and feelings across. Most LPP children learn quite early that they can derive clues from what they see around them to help them understand what is being said. Some have learned to watch a speaker's mouth for clues about what sounds are being produced.

For some children with LPP, learning to read improves their ability to manage language information. If a child can master the alphabetic code, written language offers some advantages. The words stay put. The message does not get lost the way spoken messages do. It can be read again and again. Knowing the alphabetic code also allows a listener to spell or visualize the written word as an aide to learning new words. For some children new words are stored and remembered better in this form.

However, some children with LPP do not have particularly well-developed systems for processing visual information. Some may have as much, if not more, difficulty with this kind of input. And some children with language processing problems may also experience dyslexia. They cannot easily use the alphabetic principle that enables the rest of us to translate between language sounds and the letters that encode them. And so the advantages that written language can provide are not available to these children.

11

DOES MY CHILD HAVE A LANGUAGE PROCESSING PROBLEM?

As we discovered earlier, a problem limited to language processing can not usually be detected by the language testing typically carried out at school. In addition, the symptoms of LPP are often confused with other problems such as attention deficit disorder. Thus, most children whose LPP is not accompanied by other deficits are never diagnosed. In some cases the problem is just not noticed. In others it is attributed to laziness, rudeness, or "not paying attention". Sometimes parents and teachers are aware of problems, but aren't sure what to do. Sometimes the child is the one most aware of the problem and is already calling upon available resources to compensate for her difficulties. In this section we will learn about signals that parents can watch for to help determine whether a child has a language processing problem.

Recognizing language processing problems is not always easy because no two children with LPP are just alike. There are three main factors to account for these differences. Firstly, we have seen that language processing is very complicated. Because of this complexity, there are many possible ways for efficient language processing to be interrupted. Secondly, there is considerable variability in the severity of language processing problems among children. And lastly, there is wide variation in children's ability to draw on other resources to compensate for processing problems. Thus, variation occurs because of differences in the part of the language processing system which is affected, differences in the degree of impairment and differences in the child's other abilities. In addition, these factors interact with the normal course of language development. So, children of different ages also show somewhat different symptoms of LPP.

Recognizing LPP in preschoolers

It is particularly difficult to recognize language processing disorders in preschoolers. The first four or five years of life are times of incredible change. Development in physical, intellectual, social and emotional spheres is rapid and continuous. The interaction of these separate, but related paths of development results in behaviors which are not easy to ascribe to one specific cause or another.

Language processing is a problem from day one. Remember that a newborn does not know the vocabulary or grammar of its language. Although its brain is endowed with the basic framework necessary to learn language, its only experience with language is what it has been able to gather by hearing or feeling the vibration of its mother speaking. Thus except for some familiarity with the melody of speech, the newborn has essentially no language knowledge nor experience with language processing. However, the infant's capacity to learn language leads him to engage in solving that complex puzzle during his first several years of life. Learning to process language is a problem that the infant solves little by little throughout the preschool years and beyond. So, in a sense, all preschoolers have language processing problems.

The way very young children attack the problem of understanding language is to use strategies for comprehension. One strategy for understanding language is to assume that people are talking about what they are looking at or focusing on. This is one way children learn the names of things. They associate what they hear with whatever the speaker is attending to.

Toddlers understand the here and now. When people are talking about other times and places or things that are not readily apparent they don't usually understand. Parents figure this out quickly when they have promised a special treat. "Let's have some ice cream this afternoon." Although they certainly understand "ice cream" toddlers can't wait because they don't understand concepts like "this afternoon", "tomorrow" or "next week."

Another strategy language learners use is to do what they would normally do with things. For example, if given an apple, the language learner makes the assumption that she is going to eat it. If a young child is given an apple and told to "roll the apple" she will probably bite it instead. This is perfectly normal behavior for a two-year-old child. Only later when she learns what "roll" means and can process three-word sentences that contradict normal expectations can she follow this type of instruction.

We parents are willing accomplices to comprehension strategies because we usually follow these same rules when talking to young children. If we don't they may not understand. In fact some parents are so in tune with their child's comprehension abilities that, without realizing it, they rarely say anything to their child that he can't understand. This happens most often when a child's language comprehension is not developing very rapidly. In such a situation parents often say "My child understands everything," but on reflection they realize that they never ask the child to do anything he isn't already expecting to do.

Even though all language learners have processing problems, some children have more trouble than others. Some children just get bogged down in the process of learning to use language. All young children can benefit if their parents are attuned to such problems. Being more aware of language problems gives parents a great appreciation of their child's normal communication development and leads to early detection and remediation when serious problems do occur. The following are some problems to watch for in preschoolers.

Doesn't seem to understand. Parents express this concern in many ways. "He doesn't listen." "She doesn't respond when I call her name." "He doesn't do what I ask." These are valid concerns. Anyone with a toddler or preschooler knows that they don't always listen. Sometimes they are too preoccupied with what they are doing to attend to you or they simply don't want to do what you tell them. But a child who consistently doesn't seem to hear or understand what is said to her has a real problem. This behavior may indicate a subtle hearing impairment or difficulty with language processing. It also could be indicative of social or emotional problems. Try to make note of the specific situations when the behavior occurs.

Does your child understand and respond better if he can see you talking? If so, he may be depending on visual information about speech and the speaking context to compensate for a hearing loss or language processing problem. When a hearing problem is suspected at any age, an audiological evaluation is in order.

Does your child understand better if you repeat the message or wait longer for an answer? He may need you to speak more slowly or allow extra time for him to process the message.

Will she respond if you use simpler language? In this case either the vocabulary or sentence structure may have been too difficult to be processed efficiently.

Late to talk. Language and child-development specialists expect children to be saying some single words at one year of age and to be combining words into short utterances like "Mommy bye-bye" or "Daddy car" by age two. If a child does not achieve these language milestones as expected there may be cause for concern.

Even children who appear to understand language quite well may have problems which interfere with the normal development of language output.

Young children who do not seem to understand language or are not talking as expected by two years of age should be evaluated by a speech-language pathologist. A thorough evaluation should include a hearing assessment as well as assessment of the child's level of language comprehension (understanding), his language expression, and his speech production abilities. The speech and language evaluation report should include a plan of treatment based on the results of the assessment.

Shyness, aggression and temper tantrums. All of these behaviors can occur for many reasons and are quite common in preschoolers. However we should not overlook the contribution of language processing problems to these behaviors. Many children who have difficulty thinking of words or organizing their ideas into sentences choose to remain quiet and are perceived as shy. Other children with similar language output problems but with more outgoing personalities might try to make their wishes known by physical means rather than talking. When compounded by the frustration of not being understood this physical strategy can become aggressive. Even the quiet, shy child may become unexpectedly aggressive if frustration level is high.

As we know all too well, preschoolers, even those with excellent language abilities, do have temper tantrums. Although we are not always aware of it, when we look more closely we find that they are often related to poor communication. Frequently temper tantrums occur when a child is unable to communicate what she wants or when she fails to understand a situation. A child may have unrealistic expectations because she does not know all the relevant information.

A child who seemed happy and excited at the prospect of going to a "book fair" may suddenly dissolve into tears or tantrum behavior when she arrives to find that there is no carousel as she had expected based on her experience at the "county fair". This type of letdown is fairly frequent for normal preschoolers. For the child who has difficulty processing spoken language these problems occur more frequently.

Made-up words. If a child has trouble remembering the names of things (word retrieval problems) one creative way to solve the problem is to make something up. Some children use one particular word for anything they can't think of. Others make up a variety of new words. The technical term for these new words is "neologism". There are some standard words adults use in this situation ("whatchamacallit", "thingy") but the made-up words of young children are often delightfully funny. A friend tells of the little boy who liked to visit the "zoomesum". Making up occasional words is quite normal for children, but children who depend regularly on made-up words or who can't be understood because a large proportion of their speech is "like some other language" are having language processing and/or language learning difficulties.

Otitis media. Also known as middle ear disease or ear infection, otitis media is common among preschoolers. For some the attacks are infrequent and brief, but for others ear infections occur chronically and often linger for months. When the middle ear is filled with fluid or pus, auditory signals are not transmitted faithfully to the inner ear, making it more difficult for the brain to interpret the information. Some children who suffer long periods of fluctuating hearing acuity during their early years later exhibit language processing problems or other language or learning problems. Parents need to be aware of the possibility of LPP resulting from chronic ear infections. It would be wise to take any steps that can be taken to avoid infection or reduce the symptoms during bouts of otitis media.

Recognizing LPP in school-age children.

By the time children start school they have mastered their language well enough to communicate quite effectively. During the school years they continue to add words to their vocabularies and learn to integrate ideas more fluidly in their speaking and writing. With each passing year a child understands and produces longer sentences and gradually becomes more adept at using language. From the beginning, school is linguistically demanding. In other words, a large proportion of school work depends on language skills. The walls of an elementary school classroom clearly show that visual input and hands-on experiences are an important part of learning at this stage, but at the core, listening, speaking, reading and writing are what school is about.

Many children who have managed to get along fine at home or in preschool find the language demands of school to be overwhelming. At school, being able to listen to and understand stories, instructions and discussions becomes ever more important. And to be successful at school a child must be confident enough of her language abilities to contribute information and participate in group discussions. Some of the same symptoms that parents of preschoolers observe may continue into the early school years. In addition, new symptoms of language processing problems may now appear. Again it is important for parents and teachers to be able to recognize the symptoms of LPP so that children are not made to feel inferior and are offered appropriate help. Signs of language processing problems in school-age children include:

Frequently says "huh?" or "what?". The school-age child with LPP frequently doesn't understand what she hears. If she knows she is being addressed she asks for clarification by saying "what?". Parents sometimes think this is just a habit. This opinion is often verified by the fact that the child sometimes goes on to answer the question without actually getting the clarification or repetition she seemed to be asking for. This pattern is seen when a child needs extra time for processing. She doesn't understand at first, but after a few seconds for processing to catch up she has got it pretty well figured out. But sometimes there isn't enough information available to figure it out. Then clarification or repetition really is necessary. Habitually asking "What?" does serve a purpose. It gives more time for processing and is a backup in case repetition is necessary.

My mother was often frustrated with me because I didn't answer her or said "huh?". I was well aware (at least subconsciously) that I had trouble understanding her if she wasn't looking at me. Often I did not even know that she was addressing me if I was, for example, walking ahead of her when she spoke to me. Although I sometimes asked her to look at me when she was talking, it was hard for her to remember this because she knew that there were plenty of times when I overheard things that she did not particularly want me to know. It was only much later that I realized that I regularly watched people's mouths for clues about what they were saying. If she was behind me I couldn't do it. Clearly there were times when it wasn't necessary and this must have been due to various factors. How noisy was the environment? How distracted was I by other things I was hearing, seeing or thinking? How much did I want to hear (and attend to) what she was saying? What were the important sounds and words in the message? No wonder my mother was stumped.

Misunderstands. When the LPP child knows that he hasn't understood he may ask for clarification, but sometimes he doesn't realize that he has not understood. In this case he gives an off-base answer or does the wrong thing. Those interacting with him may think him "weird" or noncompliant. And, if he realizes his error he feels embarrassed. This kind of misunderstanding often leads to problems with social interactions and to poor performance in school.

Long response time. A teacher might complain that when she asks Michael a question he just sits and stares without answering.

His parents say that he doesn't do things when he is asked to. Other children might find it hard to have a conversation with Michael. When asked a question, he looks like he is working on the answer, but he doesn't respond. Perhaps, like the child who habitually says "what?", Michael needs more time to process spoken information. If given enough time he can probably answer the question. But both he and the teacher know that only a few seconds are accorded to students to answer questions. She soon moves on to another student and Michael is relieved, but frustrated because as soon as his turn was over he knew the answer. Long response time makes social interactions difficult, especially in humourous exchanges. By the time Michael "gets the joke", the conversation has moved on and the laughter is over.

Cycle of self-consciousness. When a child is slow to respond there are several things that can be causing the problem. Processing problems may make it take longer for him to understand the question or to find the words needed to respond. However, many children (and adults) become nervous and self-conscious when in the hot seat of being required to respond, especially in front of a group. The mental processes of wondering how you will seem to others, whether your answer is correct, or if your ideas are worthwhile, not to mention thinking about why you can't think of the right words, take up the processing capacity you could be using to solve the problem posed. In ordinary interactions the time allowed for responses is fairly short and tends to exacerbate the self-consciousness problem. I call this the self-consciousness cycle because after only one or a few experiences having trouble answering in class, self-consciousness can become a habit. And the habit of self-consciousness further interferes with efficient language processing.

Can't think of words. Word retrieval problems continue to occur at all ages for many people with LPP. While preschoolers often make up words, school-age children who can't find the words they want use a variety of strategies to compensate. They may just stall or say that they can't think of the word. Some children have learned to talk their way around the concept they are trying to get across (we call this circumlocution). Or they may use a made-up word; now often a conventional one such as "thingy". Sometimes they will use a word which is close in meaning but not quite what they mean. Some children use words which are similar in some ways but do not mean the same thing, for example saying "volcano" instead of "tornado". And sometimes children use words that they have misremembered or misheard, for example "rememberized" for "memorized". Because learning new words usually involves encountering them several times and none of us has exactly the same experiences, we each store vocabulary somewhat differently. Thus we may never really know what makes a child use a particular word for another. However naming errors provide fertile ground for researchers trying to determine how we learn, store and retrieve vocabulary.

Pauses and fillers. Pauses and space-fillers (e.g., "um", "well", "uh", "and so", "like", etc.) and also repetitions and reformulations of words and phrases may interrupt a child's flow of speech. These interruptions of the normal flow of speech are termed "mazes". Organizing long, complicated sentences or stories requires skillful use of language. When children have difficulty organizing what they want to say, their speech tends to be broken up by these intrusions. Sometimes mazes result from confusion and revision and sometimes they are used to "hold the floor" giving the speaker more time to organize what he has to say. Difficulties with fluid expression may arise from word retrieval problems, from poor knowledge of grammatical structure or from uncertainty about the order of events or amount of information to provide.

Excessive talking. One unexpected symptom of language processing problems is excessive talking. The engaging little chatterbox who is constantly talking may be putting up a smokescreen. As long as she is in control of the conversation she is fine. She is talking about familiar things and knows what to say. However, if you begin to question her, her responses may be delayed or off the mark and you will probably observe lots of mazes. If you pay close attention you may also notice that the excessive talker often uses circumlocution. Circumlocution means that she describes things and uses vague references rather than using precise vocabulary. This is one common solution to word retrieval problems. Another possible reason for excessive talking is the child's need to "talk through" an idea to really understand it. This may be something like reading the instructions out loud when putting together a new bicycle or computer system.

Trouble learning to read. If your child has adequate language knowledge and normal vision and is having more trouble than his classmates learning to read, you can be fairly sure that he is having trouble at some level with language processing. His problem may be specific to reading. Some children whose spoken language skills seem quite normal, have great difficulty learning to read. This specific difficulty with reading is usually called dyslexia, although some schools have more precise definitions for the term or avoid using it altogether.

Very often the real problem is one of phonological memory, which is the ability to remember speech sounds. This could mean having trouble remembering which sound goes with which symbol. But the problem may not only be with making associations between letters and their sounds. Another problem in learning to read is sounding out new words. There the problem is to remember the sequence of letter sounds that you have just decoded long enough to get to the end of the word. When a child has this kind of problem remembering speech sounds you might also find that, when speaking, he has difficulty learning new, multi-syllabic words or repeating made-up words, especially if they are long. Consistent mispronunciation of newly learned names is a sign of a phonological memory problem and is often associated with reading problems.

Tires easily. Is your child completely exhausted when she comes home from school? Some children with language processing problems have discovered ways to compensate for their difficulties, but this may mean that they are working much harder than others to keep up with the class. A common result is a child who can concentrate on school work for a certain period, but then must have a rest. Recess helps, as does switching to some completely nonverbal task, but the structure of school usually doesn't allow for breaks as frequently as some LPP children need them. Thus teachers often see a child "shut down" and just not be able to do any more of a particular task. Some LPP children fall asleep during class and I have met some children who need a daily nap after school.

Math difficulty. At first it is hard to understand how language processing problems could affect math performance. In fact, many children with LPP show superior abilities in computation and the visual/spatial problem solving which is most often thought of as mathematics. However, many aspects of math depend on verbal comprehension and memory. Even at the most basic level the names of numbers must be remembered. More commonly children have trouble remembering basic math facts, for example the sum of 8 plus 7 or the result of 11 minus 4.

While this causes some problems, many children spontaneously realize that they can count on their fingers or use other strategies to get the answer. It is a bit slower, but very accurate. I have personal experience with visions of humanized, animated numbers whose interactions always produced predictable results, giving me the answers to simple math problems. And I have talked to other adults who remember similar and even more bizarre strategies for doing math.

But the contribution of language to math does not end with remembering names for numbers and sums. In third or fourth grade word problems rear their ugly heads. Being able to remember the relevant factors and work through a problem written out in sentence or paragraph form stresses language processing much more than doing problems set down in mathematical format.

Even doing typical math problems requires a significant amount of verbal processing capacity. One of the basic skills of math is to learn procedures. After learning the basics of addition and subtraction, children must learn procedures for carrying and borrowing, for multiplying large numbers and doing long division, and for working with fractions. The procedures are usually taught and remembered verbally as a set of instructions. First do this, then do this, etc. Until he has truly learned and integrated these procedures into his knowledge about math the LPP child will be stumped at times because he can't retrieve the procedure from his memory.

Recognizing LPP in high school students

As children proceed in school from the early grades to middle school and high school, reliance on language skill continues to increase. Some children who have managed to perform adequately in grade school begin to develop problems as oral and written language demands become greater. In the upper grades children must process not only a greater volume of language information, but must manage a larger vocabulary, longer sentences and more complex grammatical structures. Weaknesses in verbal memory, word retrieval, organization or processing speed that were insignificant before may now become apparent. Below are some signs of difficulty to be aware of in junior and senior high school students. Remember, this is just a guideline. Some of these problems may occur at earlier ages and some of the problems mentioned in the previous section may continue.

More math difficulty. By junior high school many finger counters have gotten very proficient, but word problems are getting even harder and there are new and more complicated procedures to learn. Many bright LPP students solve problems in algebra or geometry by creative processes such as analogy, successive approximation, intuition or by resorting to first principles and recreating the procedures from scratch because they can't remember the steps. While they often get the correct answer, these processes are usually time consuming and exhausting. On the other hand, some of them yield good answers faster than the prescribed methods.

It should be noted that some LPP children do very well on standardized math tests where several possible answers are provided. Starting with the provided answers and using a process of elimination to narrow down the field can be quite effective when one is practiced at alternative problem solving. Depending on how successful his methods are the LPP child will feel more or less confident in math, but even the successful ones think that they are "cheating" by not using the standard methods.

Uses the wrong word or says words incorrectly. Although younger children often do these things, the larger vocabulary required of high school students can make this problem more apparent. This category overlaps with those above regarding word retrieval and phonological memory. Problems with phonological memory can cause the sound sequence of a new word to be remembered and pronounced incorrectly. Some students use a wrong word because they have learned the wrong meaning for a particular sound sequence or have confused two or more similar sounding words and retrieved the wrong one for the occasion.

Test anxiety. Test anxiety is directly related to a student's confidence, whether it be in math, science, social studies or language. Many students who are able to use information and explain concepts under certain circumstances find that in the context of a test they are unable to remember or express what they know that they know. Perhaps the time constraints, the lack of any useful reference or the requirement to produce on demand interfere with the ability to remember and process effectively. At any rate, experiencing the panic of not remembering interferes further with memory and processing. After this has happened a few times a self-fulfilling prophecy can be set up. If processing capacity is taken up worrying about not remembering the answers, the student will be less able to focus and less able to retrieve the information he wants.

Subtle problems with grammar. By the time a child is in junior or senior high school language problems which result in consistent errors with basic grammar should already have been addressed. However, problems using complex syntactic structures for integrating clauses and phrases into logical sentences are often overlooked. Many children with LPP have difficulty learning to use subordinating conjunctions (for example, unless, whether, although, until, whenever) and relative pronouns (for example, who, which, that) correctly to produce complex sentences. For example, LPP students are rarely heard to use sentences like "My home room teacher, who recently returned from a trip to the Far East, is giving a talk and slide show tomorrow night," or "Unless every student in the 8th grade has turned in a book report there will be no class trip". Sometimes LPP students use these connecting words incorrectly but more often they just don't use them at all. Instead they stick to shorter sentences with less complex phrase and clause structure. We use subordinating conjunctions and relative pronouns to show the relationship between two or more ideas. They allow an adept language user to integrate ideas very efficiently. But in order to use these words correctly a speaker must understand where they can be used and their shades of meaning. Because these connecting words usually occur in fairly long sentences it can be difficult for a person with limited available working memory to learn their meaning well enough to be able to use them correctly when producing sentences.

Comprehension. LPP students sometimes report problems understanding written and spoken language. For the most part they have trouble when sentences are very long or use complex syntactic structures as mentioned just above. Listening to speech which is too rapid also compromises comprehension for many students. In addition, many students, even those who have easily mastered the mechanics of reading, have particular difficulty comprehending what they read. They may have to reread a paragraph many times before the words really sink in.

Choice of sports. Sport is another area, like mathematics, which initially seems to be more or less unaffected by language. We rarely attend to the fact that many sports require a great deal of communication to be successfully played. In general, team sports require good communication between players. One player's failure to understand the coach's directions or his delay in understanding a team member's signal could cause problems for the whole team. Many children with LPP are quite athletic and skillful in sports, but over the years, I have observed that they tend to prefer sports where they compete alone rather than as part of a team. Many LPP students I have known are excellent swimmers, skiers, tennis players, etc., but they often report that do not enjoy team sports.

12

WHAT IF MY CHILD HAS A LANGUAGE PROCESSING PROBLEM?

No single child with a language processing problem will exhibit all of the signs described in the previous chapter. And there are other possible causes for some of the symptoms. But, suppose you have become familiar with the warning signs and recognize that your child exhibits some of them, then what should you do about it?

Getting an evaluation

If your child is a preschooler his speech and language should be evaluated by a certified speech-language pathologist. It is important that his hearing be tested in conjunction with the evaluation. Preschoolers with symptoms of language problems should have a professional evaluation as soon as possible because early speech, language and hearing treatment is very effective. Failure to provide early treatment can lead to more severe problems which will require longer treatment. Later treatment may also be less effective. The American Speech-Language-Hearing Association (ASHA) certifies speech-language pathologists and audiologists (hearing specialists) by awarding the Certificate of Clinical Competence. Choose a qualified CCC-holding professional to evaluate your child. You can recognize a certified practitioner by the initials CCC-SLP (speech and language) or CCC-A (audiology, i.e., hearing) after his or her name.

If your child is older and you think the problems she is having are mild, you may want to skip to Chapters 14 to 17 and implement some of the treatment suggestions made there before resorting to a professional evaluation. However, at any age, if your child is struggling and frustrated and is not receiving appropriate help with her problem it would be wise to schedule a language evaluation with a speech-language pathologist. If school language testing has not found a language disorder but you continue to suspect language processing problems be sure you schedule your child's evaluation with a speech-language pathologist who is familiar with test procedures to isolate language processing disorders. While you are waiting for your appointment it may be helpful to try some of the suggestions listed in Chapters 14 to 17. If you make careful observations of your child's response you will be able to add important information to the evaluation process.

When making the appointment for a school-age child you should ask to speak with the speech-language pathologist who will be carrying out the evaluation. Make it clear to her that you are concerned about on-line language processing and ask if she will use measures which specifically explore on-line language processing abilities.

As we learned, language knowledge and language processing are closely tied and it is difficult to separate them. While deficits in language processing may affect language knowledge and vice versa, we know it is very possible to have good language knowledge and still have trouble with on-line language processing.

Most of the language tests routinely administered to children during language assessments are designed to diagnose disorders of overall language understanding and use and do not specifically single out on-line language processing. If your child's vocabulary, general knowledge and basic grammatical skills are good the evaluation may reveal only that she "was slow to respond" or "has essentially normal language skills with some difficulty repeating sen-

tences" etc. So a general language evaluation will probably not be
able to specifically delineate the factors affecting your school-age
child's language processing problem and thus may not provide
useful recommendations.

While administering standardized tests the competent speech-
language pathologist makes observations about how a child responds, noting delays, self-corrections, etc. Thus, many language
tests, when used by a professional familiar with the distinction
between language knowledge and language processing, can indicate difficulties in specific areas of processing. However, because
most tests score only the content of responses and do not quantify
the processing factors, they cannot provide clear, quantifiable evidence for a deficit in language processing. In most cases, a child
must achieve a score significantly below the established mean on
one or more tests to be considered for any remedial services at
school. In order to meet these criteria, the test must directly measure the child's problem area.

A thorough evaluation to isolate an on-line language processing problem, does need to include measures of both language processing and language knowledge. Results from tests of vocabulary
and grammatical knowledge serve to rule out a more encompass-
ing language disorder and to provide data for a comparison between language knowledge and language processing skills. The
evaluation may also include a brief test of nonverbal intelligence if
IQ scores are not available from other sources. In addition to gaining information about general intelligence and language knowledge the evaluation of a school-age child should include one or
more measures which address on-line language processing directly.

There are some language measures currently available which
focus specifically on processing. A few are commercially available
and others are published in research journals. What makes these
tests good at assessing language processing? The goal of these measures is to control or equate vocabulary and grammatical structure
across items while varying the processing load. In this way they
can illuminate the efficiency of processing while minimizing the

impact of previous knowledge about language on the results of the test. Of course they are still language tests and so words cannot be deleted, but these tests use nonsense words or a small vocabulary of commonly used words so that previous knowledge of vocabulary is of negligible importance to the result. The amount of information to be processed is an important factor and thus the length of the test items is often manipulated as a variable in the testing.

There are a few measures which I find particularly useful for identifying language processing problems. They measure different aspects of processing. I choose which to use based on the kinds of problems the child has been experiencing. Unfortunately none of these measures can be used with very young children. Another shortcoming is that some of the measures have been used mainly as research tools. Thus they have not been widely administered and therefore do not have norms based on large populations. In spite of these drawbacks, I have found them extremely useful in clearly pinpointing and documenting specific language processing problems.

Tests of language processing

The *Revised Token Test (RTT)* is one of the most useful measures for assessing the processing of language input. It is particularly helpful in evaluating children who have difficulty following directions and remembering verbal information. It consists of spoken instructions to be carried out with a set of plastic tokens. The simplest instructions are of the form "Touch the red circle". But instructions become both longer "Touch the red circle and the blue square" and more complex "Put the red circle above the blue square" in an organized and gradual way. The child's responses are evaluated using a sophisticated scoring system which takes into account the promptness, certainty, completeness and accuracy of each part of the response and makes note of strategies the child uses when responding. Quantifying the errors, strategies and un-certainties that come into play during the response is very instructive in understanding a child's language processing problem. The detailed scoring system allows for careful analysis of the importance for a given child of the factors which increase processing load.

The *RTT* is available commercially, however the test includes normative data only for people age 17 and over. Some preliminary normative data based on a fairly small sample of children from age 5 through 12 is available from the author, Malcolm McNeil, at the Department of Communication Science and Disorders, University of Pittsburgh.

Some other forms of the token test are available, including at least one designed for children. But most of them do not make a strong effort to control the length and complexity of commands and do not use a multidimensional scoring system. Thus they are more difficult to interpret and can not be used as easily to pinpoint specific strengths and weaknesses.

In the area of phonological memory, nonsense word repetition tasks are the best measures available. Researchers both here and in the United Kingdom, have shown that non-word repetition tasks have considerable power to differentiate between children with and without language disorders. Repeating nonsense words makes direct demands on phonological memory. By not using actual words, these tasks prevent familiarity and previous learning from affecting the results. Dollaghan and Campbell's version of the task uses a particularly well-constructed set of nonsense words. Equal numbers of words, one to four syllables in length, have been created specifically to maximize perceptibility, minimize articulation problems and ensure that the repetition is not affected by previous vocabulary knowledge.

One measure I developed with Tom Campbell for exploring the dimensions of children's language processing difficulties is the *Competing Language Processing Test (CLPT)*. The *CLPT* measures working memory by testing how well a child can manage two kinds of language processing simultaneously. In other words, how effectively can the child allocate limited processing resources to two competing tasks? It requires children to answer simple yes/no questions while at the same time remembering certain words to be repeated later. This test puts a significant burden on working memory, but it reflects many real-life situations. For example, the task is very similar to situations in which you must remember specific information while continuing to listen to instructions or carry on a conversation. Many times a child's performance on this test will show deficiencies compared to same-age children even when other language processing tests have revealed no problems.

There are also several good ways to judge the efficiency of output processing. The *Test of Word Finding* and the *Test of Adolescent/ Adult Word Finding* are commercially-available naming tests which are used to quantify word retrieval proficiency. They measure both speed and accuracy of naming and provide an analysis of error types which is very helpful in categorizing word retrieval problems.

Assessing children's spontaneous output of sentences is also important. Standard language evaluations should (but often do not) include a measure of the average length of a child's spontaneous spoken sentences. This is typically termed mean length of utterance (MLU) or mean length of communication unit (MLCU). The procedure involves tape-recording a sample of the child's narrative (telling or retelling a story, movie or TV show plot or describing an event from life). The tape is then transcribed and the transcript analyzed. The number of words per sentence or utterance can be compared to various available standards. The transcript can also be used to assess the use of grammatical structures and vocabulary.

It is particularly important that a language sample be recorded when language processing is the main concern. It is sometimes found that children with LPP use shorter sentences than other children their age even though that was not originally a concern. And, although few grammatical errors may be observed in their speech, some LPP children tend to use only fairly simple grammatical structures.

However, for most LPP children, the really notable result of language sample analysis is the large number of mazes used. I like to analyze narrative transcripts using Loban's guidelines particularly because he provides a method for assessing the percentage of a child's words which occur in mazes.

One test of general communication ability which serves well in evaluating children with LPP is the *Porch Index of Communicative Abilities in Children*. A great advantage is that it can be administered to children as young as 3 years of age. Like the RTT it uses a very restricted vocabulary and has a multi-dimensional scoring system which adds to its interpretive power. It provides very specific information about performance in a number of communicative modalities (listening, speaking, reading, writing) and can be used to recognize language processing problems. A disadvantage is that this test may only be administered by professionals who have undergone an intensive training program.

If no other measure is available, tests of sentence imitation can give some indication of difficulty with verbal working memory. However, it must be remembered that many factors such as familiarity of vocabulary, grammatical complexity and sentence meaning will affect performance on this type of measure.

While this section has been a bit technical I hope it will help you make the most of your child's language processing evaluation.

Do children with LPP need special services?

Many children with LPP will need to have a language and hearing evaluation to pinpoint their problems and make specific recommendations for ways to improve performance. This is especially true if the child is very young or is experiencing significant difficulty or frustration with language.

When recommendations are made, how will they be implemented? Who will provide the treatment? Will speech-language therapy help? The answers to these questions depend on the findings of the evaluation.

While there are many important things parents and teachers can do to help, the speech-language pathologist's expertise is invaluable in solving certain problems. For example, she can develop a step-by-step program for teaching new language skills and devise plans for practicing the new forms to increase the automaticity of their use. Speech-language pathologists are trained to work at all levels of language, from sounds, to words, to sentences and narrative. They can help improve processing at all levels. In addition a speech-language pathologist can help identify the most effective strategies families can use to improve a particular child's language processing and work to help families incorporate these strategies into their day-to-day interactions.

If your child's language processing problems are severe or are accompanied by problems with language knowledge, then speech-language therapy will be a necessary part of his developmental and educational program. Both language knowledge and language processing should be addressed in treatment, though the emphasis on each will depend on the child's specific difficulties.

Special attention should be paid to toddlers and preschoolers with language problems. Because language development is normally occurring so rapidly at this age, any neurological problem which might interfere with language learning should be addressed as soon as possible. Early intervention services are incredibly important in giving young children the right start and in helping families to understand what to expect and how to help their child develop to his or her full potential..

For other children with LPP, a variety of treatment arrangements are possible. When the main problem is with reading, a reading specialist will probably be the best person to provide intervention. Most other language processing problems are addressed by a speech-language pathologist, language arts teacher or special education teacher. Many children with LPP will need only a brief period of treatment to help them understand their problem or problems and develop effective strategies to overcome them. As the problems change with changes in language demands in higher grades, a further brief period of therapy may be necessary.

Many children have language processing problems which are quite mild. Some of these children won't need any professional treatment. They have already developed effective strategies. They need only to be given credit for their ingenuity and encouraged to use their strategies and to develop new ones as new problems arise.

Parents want to know how to fix the language processing problems they see in their children. If only there was a pill or magic cure that would end the problems for good. Of course we don't have such a wonder drug. Instead we have a little knowledge (more and more every year) about how the brain works and some research into what kinds of treatment can help people's brains function more effectively.

In the following chapters I discuss some ideas gleaned from research and from my own experience which have been found helpful in working with children with language processing problems. In addition to ideas for parents and teachers I have included some information about the types of treatment programs which speech-language pathologists and researchers have found to be effective in addressing particular aspects of disordered language processing.

13
HOW CAN I HELP?

Whether your child's language processing problem is mild or severe, isolated or part of a more global language disorder, there are things you can do to make life easier for your child and everyone around her. Some of the suggestions provided in chapters 14 through 17 are general and broad in their effect and will enhance language processing for any listener. Others are quite specific and will be applicable only to certain children. I have tried to present the most generally important or helpful ideas first with ideas for more specific problems toward the end of each section. Often you will not know if a particular solution will help your child until you try it for a while. Deciding which to use will depend on the severity of your child's language problems, the specific areas of difficulty, the personalities of those involved and your own family routine and patterns of interaction.

There are several ways to approach language processing problems and I definitely believe in attacking from all directions. Even if your child does not require speech-language therapy you can make a significant impact on her performance and self-esteem. Implementation of external and internal strategies is very effective in improving language processing. External strategies involve making changes in the environment and in the language input the child receives. These strategies are most often used by parents and teachers to reduce processing demands for children, making it easier for them to succeed in communicative interactions.

Internal strategies are routines that children can learn that make language processing work more effectively. Some of these strategies may seem like shortcuts or tricks, but they are used everyday by successful people to manage the language demands they encounter. LPP children often figure out some useful internal strategies for themselves but learning new ones can give them a big boost in performance. Some children just need to know that it is okay (not cheating) to use strategies.

In the next four chapters I lay out recommendations for strategies to be used by parents, teachers and children themselves. But before we get to the specific things you can do to help, I want to set the stage for working with your child on communication.

In striving to improve school performance and social interactions, many parents become entirely focused on whether their child is succeeding. They often forget to look at their child as a whole. Each child is a separate individual with strengths, weaknesses, particular skills, interests and gifts which are his alone. For many children school skills and particularly language are not strengths. This can make them feel inadequate, uninterested and even depressed about school. But all children have something to offer, some special talent or ability whether it be in sport or art or in making others smile. It is very important that parents and teachers help children find their special abilities and make sure that these abilities are nurtured and appreciated. The child who feels badly about himself will have much less energy to work on improving language than the child who knows that he is worthwhile and appreciated.

In my experience evaluating children with language processing problems I have repeatedly found that often all that is needed to make a huge improvement in a child's performance and a family's interaction is to explain the problem to the child and the family. This works especially well with children age 10 or 11 and above. Very often the child feels stupid and inadequate. She is using some strategies but feels like she is cheating and not doing things the way others are. Parents are often baffled and frustrated. They may believe that their child is just lazy and have tried various ways to get her to perform better, always meeting with failure. Oftentimes, as soon as parents and students understand the nature of the problem they begin to formulate their own plans about how to solve it. The student is relieved to find that he is not "dumb" and feels assured that the strategies he is using are on target and that there are more he can try. The parents see why the measures they have tried before don't work and are eager to try some new ways of approaching the problem.

My recommendations are divided into four chapters, corresponding to the four main categories of language processing that children seem to have difficulty with: listening and following directions, remembering sounds and words, word finding, and organizing language output. There is definitely some overlap between areas and some suggestions work well for more than one problem.

I have further divided each chapter into three sections. The first, external strategies, includes suggestions which are mainly for parents and teachers to implement. Internal strategies are suggestions which children themselves (especially older students) can try using. The third section includes proven treatment programs which should be used under the supervision of a speech-language pathologist or an educational professional. Again, there will be some overlap between categories.

The lists are long, but don't be overwhelmed. Try picking out 2 or 3 ideas to try. You should see some changes after implementing a suggestion for a week or two. Gradually add other ideas that seem like they might work and delete ones that don't seem to help. You will want to share this information with others who work with your child (teachers, therapists, day-care providers) so that they can try using the strategies, too. Try to observe what causes the biggest problems for your child and pick remedies which address these issues.

14

SUGGESTIONS FOR IMPROVING LISTENING AND FOLLOWING DIRECTIONS

External strategies: What parents and teachers can do to help.

Preview events. This is one of the most important changes you can make, especially for young children. It means telling your child, beforehand, what is going to happen. This is particularly necessary when life is not going by the normal routine. If your child is going to a new place or going to meet someone new, talk to her about what to expect. What kind of place is it, how will you get there, how long will it take, who will be there, what kind of things might happen and what might she be expected to do or say. Knowing about things ahead of time allows a child to prepare and not be overwhelmed by the processing demands of a new experience. It means that she will be more able to listen and better able to understand in the new situation. Equally important, knowing what to expect will reduce the bewilderment and/or temper tantrums that many children exhibit when suddenly asked to perform in a new, confusing and unexplored situation. Previewing is easy to do but we often forget to let our children in on our plans. It is a good habit to get into with children even before you think they can understand much of what you are saying. They understand more than you think and you'll be surprised how previewing helps life go smoothly. Older children also appreciate having some background for new places and events.

Get your child's attention. If your child's mind is engaged in something, whether it be getting dressed, building with blocks, watching a video or just daydreaming, it will be hard for him to process directions from you. Get your child's attention before saying what you want him to hear. There are many ways to get a child's attention. Just calling his name does not ensure that you have it.

Reduce distractions. Noisy and distracting environments make language processing difficult. While it is not always possible to achieve complete calm and quiet, it is worth working toward peaceful surroundings. When noise and distractions are a problem it is even more important to use the following strategies.

Look at your listener. Making eye contact usually ensures you have a child's attention. But don't require a child to keep looking at your eyes while you are talking. Some children will need to watch your mouth for visual cues to help with language processing. And many people listen and remember more effectively when looking slightly away from the speaker (usually down and to the left). Even if a child is not looking directly at you, don't turn your back. Your listener may need to refer to your face and your voice should be directed toward him. Teachers who talk while writing on the blackboard risk having many students miss what they are saying.

Be clear. If you speak clearly it will be much easier for listeners with LPP (and everyone else) to process your message. But, speaking clearly is not a simple matter. There are a number of factors involved in clear speech. The *content* should be to the point and not rambling. The *vocabulary* should be appropriate to your audience and the *sentence structure* straightforward. Your *rate* of speech should be fairly slow and your *enunciation* should be precise.

Repeat what you have said. Depending on the type of communication you are engaging in, it may be helpful to restate what you have said. This could take the form of summarizing your expectations, going over steps, clarifying details or simply repeating. When explaining something new, it is a good idea to go over the information three times. First tell what you are going to explain, explain it well and then summarize what should have been learned. Don't just repeat yourself over and over, however. It's just a waste of breath. Make sure you have the child's attention, then if she doesn't seem to understand, simplify what you are saying until you reach a level your child comprehends.

Use non-verbal supports. Gestures and facial expressions can help make your point. Or provide pictures, objects and demonstration to help with explanations or directions. For older children it is helpful if teachers can provide a written outline of the material to be covered in class, in advance. That way the student (and parent) can look over the outline and be better prepared to understand the new material when it is presented.

Allow time. Even with careful presentation of information, some children need a bit longer for processing than others. Be willing to wait for the child's response. Discourage siblings and classmates from rushing to fill the conversational gap. They, too, can learn to wait a bit in their interactions with the LPP child.

Encourage requests for clarification. Repeat readily if your child asks you to. Restate what you have said to make it more easily understandable. If you think your child has not understood, do clarify and let her know that asking for more information is a good way to understand better.

Internal strategies: What children can learn to do to help themselves.

Be ready for directions. There are times and places when it is more likely that instructions will be given. A child can learn to recognize these situations and be attentive to the person in charge and ready to listen.

Ask for repetition or clarification. If he is not sure he has understood what to do, the child should learn to ask for help. Unfortunately, children are often unaware that they have not understood. A child should learn to check from time to time to be sure that what he is doing makes sense and is what he is supposed to do.

Repeat directions. Children can learn to say the directions back to their parent or teacher or to themselves to be sure that they heard correctly (clarifying any misunderstandings in the process).

Write it down. Using words or simple pictures, make notes about directions or the steps in a procedure and refer to them while carrying out the directions or procedure.

For students in high school, learning to take notes is a must. Develop a consistent system for taking notes and read over the day's class notes each day. That way you will be able to think about what was said and will know what questions to ask the next day. Remember to leave a wide margin when taking notes so that you can add information to clarify, integrate and comment on what you have written. If your teacher has provided a written outline of main points, that is a good place to make further notes for clarification.

Visualize. Children can learn to use their visual imaginations to help remember stories, anecdotes, directions, procedures, etc., by "making a movie" in their minds as the information is presented.

Enumerate. When learning a list of items or instructions, a child can count out the items on his fingers. Knowing how many items there are makes it easier to know when he has remembered them all. And enumeration can work with visualization so that when he looks at each finger he associates it with a particular item in the original list.

Watch speakers. When people are talking, they often give clues about what they are saying by using gestures or by pointing to what they are talking about. They also give clues about the words they are saying by the movements they make with their mouths. Children can learn to pay attention to these helpful cues and use them to help sort out the stream of sounds they are hearing. Watching speakers' mouths for cues is called speech reading.

Tape record lectures. In high school, when teachers begin to use lecture as a primary mode of teaching, it may be helpful for LPP students to tape record the lectures. Listening and taking notes simultaneously is a difficult processing task. The tape recording allows difficult passages to be reviewed later, as necessary, to complete written note taking. Another advantage of tape recording is that, after taking notes in class and becoming familiar with any new vocabulary and concepts, the student can replay the tape and listen with a prepared mind to what the lecturer is saying.

The speech-language pathologist's role in improving listening and following directions.

Many children learn some of the strategies outlined above without therapy, but sometimes children need help implementing strategies successfully. The speech-language pathologist can teach children processing strategies and evaluate which ones work best for each child.

One very important prerequisite for following directions accurately is being able to recognize whether or not you have understood the message. Chris Dollaghan and Nomi Kaston investigated the ability of young children with language disorders to monitor their comprehension of instructions. Using a graded program they successfully taught children to evaluate whether they had understood instructions and to use appropriate requests for clarification when they had not.

Another way a speech-language pathologist can help is by teaching speech reading skills. She can help a child learn the mouth movements associated with various classes of speech sounds and can provide activities for practicing speech reading and evaluating the child's success. Learning to use such visual cues to enhance speech perception improves language processing.

In the past several years research on timing difficulties in auditory and phonological perception has resulted in a new type of treatment. Fast ForWord® is a computer-based treatment program that has been shown to increase language comprehension scores of at least some language-impaired children. The program works by initially increasing the length of the very short sound transitions that distinguish similar sounds. Thus it is easier to recognize specific speech sounds. The training program then gradually shortens the transition time as the child's performance improves. To the extent that a mild language processing problem may be the result of a deficit in speech sound discrimination or phonological encoding these programs may also be helpful for children with LPP. The most impressive improvements seem to occur for children who take part in intensive training for many hours per day for several weeks. Another computer program, Earobics®, also focuses on improving phonological awareness and language processing skills.

There are also non-computerized treatment programs which have been shown to be effective in increasing children's language processing. Some of these programs appeal to the recognition that mothers, in particular, and people in general, speak differently when addressing very young children. This type of talking, which is usually slow and includes significant modulation of vocal pitch and stress, is termed "Motherese". The assumption is that the speech changes of motherese help the young child attend to important aspects of language and make language processing easier. Sandra McKinnis and Molly Thompson describe a face-to-face therapy program they have developed. "Altered Auditory Input" (AAI) involves altering verbal input to language-impaired children by varying the speed, prosody and pausing patterns. The amount and type of variation is individualized for each patient to obtain the best comprehension outcome. The authors have found that this method, in conjunction with a graded set of stimulus materials that elicits increasingly longer and more complex utterances, has had positive effects on their patients' language processing.

15

SUGGESTIONS FOR IMPROVING VERBAL MEMORY

Verbal memory covers a very broad landscape. A child could have trouble remembering the sequence of sounds in a new word or the words to a song or rhyme. Some children have trouble remembering lists or telephone numbers and others can't accurately repeat a sentence they have just heard. Being able to remember sequences of sounds and words is incredibly important to our use of language but also to learning in academic areas. The ability to rapidly recall numbers in sequence or basic math facts is the basis for further mathematical development. These fundamentals need to be available for use rapidly and automatically, leaving the bulk of processing capacity free to manage higher levels of problem solving. The problems of verbal memory overlap with some of those addressed in the previous and following sections and some of the same solutions are recommended.

External strategies: What parents and teachers can do to help.

Be understanding. Memory problems are frustrating for all involved. Children with LPP may have consistent difficulty remembering verbal material or just have irritating memory lapses. Their difficulty remembering sounds can have a pervasive effect on learning to read. Or they may temporarily forget their school principal's name, the state where they live or the procedure for doing long division. These children often need reminders. They also need patience, understanding and support in learning and using the strategies that will help them perform more effectively. Be a source of help and encouragement in a world that does not always understand.

Ask specific rather than general questions. Asking "What did you do in school today?", or "How are things going?" may elicit only a vague response because these questions don't necessarily trigger specific memories. However, this does not mean that the memories are not there. You may need to ask specifically about what happened in a certain class or with a certain person to tap into your child's memory of the school day. Another good way to get a child to talk about her day is to start the conversation by saying something about your day.

Facilitate practice. Find ways to encourage repetitive practice of important information. With young children practice counting daily during chores such as putting away toys or setting the table. Encourage children to learn the words to songs and rhymes. Those with actions are often easiest to remember. For older children make games out of reciting math facts, verb conjugations, state capitals, etc.

Analyze the problem. Pay attention to just what kinds of things your child has trouble remembering. Does he remember better if there is a rhyme or song structure? If so, turning new information into songs might help with remembering it. If rhyme and rhythm don't seem to help his memory, then don't push it. Try something else, like making visual or other associations. One child was only able to remember color names in connection with specific objects, "Red like an apple", "Yellow like the sun", etc.

Use consistent context. When learning new skills the whole experience may be connected. If Tom learns subtraction with borrowing at a particular desk in a certain room using yellow lined paper, he will probably remember the process best if he is tested under the same conditions. With enough practice he will be able to take this skill into new situations. LPP children often need more practice and a more gradual process of moving from one context to another when learning new material.

Provide cues. If the LPP child has trouble thinking of a name or phone number, give a hint of the beginning sound or first digit. Visual cues can also be helpful, for example, cue letter sounds by forming your mouth for the production of that sound. Helping the child get started is often all that is necessary to activate his memory. And by giving cues you are helping the child to develop self-cuing strategies.

Provide physical props. As soon as children can understand them, introduce memory helpers like lists, charts, schedules, calendars, etc. If charts use pictures instead of words, even young children can use them to help them remember to do daily activities. As children get older they can learn to use schedules for classes and after-school activities, reducing confusion and memory demands. Provide clear information about appointments, assignments and expectations so that students can record them in their schedules or assignment books. Writing assignments on the blackboard is particularly helpful.

Make information meaningful. New information which is interesting and relevant to students is better understood, learned and remembered. Use examples which make sense to children and which are easy to remember. With good examples, the child can retrieve or recreate the learned information when he needs it. Too often school learning involves memorizing a formula to do something which the student doesn't understand. This type of "learning" will not be as useful in the long run.

Internal strategies: What children can learn to do to help themselves.

Rehearse. Rehearsing or repeating information to oneself helps memory in the short term and can also help get verbal information into long term storage. Rehearsing rote information such as counting sequences or important information (address, telephone number, etc) amounts to practice. Practice makes processes happen more automatically, that is, more rapidly and with less demand on working memory resources.

Chunk information. Increase the size of the information bit to be remembered so that fewer items need to be stored. With phone numbers we tend to chunk the first 3 digits and then the next 4 digits so we remember just 2 chunks instead of 7 digits. Another way of chunking is to categorize items. For example, a grocery list could be divided up by aisle or food type. A list including apples, chicken, bananas, cereal, milk, carrots, eggs, bread and ground beef could be remembered more easily if divided into produce, meat and breakfast. Chunking can also be used to reduce the strain of remembering a long string of speech sounds when sounding out a new word. Learn to look at the word to see if there are any small, familiar words in it. Interpreting these as chunks rather than trying to remember all the separate letter sounds usually makes sounding out new words easier.

Use visual imagery. Making up funny visual images is often recommended to help remember people's names. Visualization can also be used to remember long lists and other kinds of information by connecting the items together in an imagined scene. In addition to just picturing what you want to remember there are a number of fancier methods for remembering long lists which involve pegging the items to be remembered to a predetermined, ordered set of items which is already memorized and always used for this purpose.

Make use of props. As children mature they can make use of various kinds of memory helpers. Why waste precious memory capacity holding on to information that could be written down? Students with language processing problems who are in the habit of using an assignment book or day planner will experience fewer memory-related catastrophes than those who aren't. LPP children who learn to make notes, write lists and maintain schedules and calendars during the school years will be more organized and will be establishing valuable habits for their lifetime.

Read it out loud. If you have trouble comprehending and remembering what you read, try reading out loud to yourself. Hearing the words, or maybe just making the mouth movements to produce the words, seems to help the information register in memory better than just looking at the words silently. You will probably feel more comfortable doing this in your own room than in the library or classroom, but even muttering the words quietly can help. Some students find that if they read into a tape recorder and then listen to what they have read helps their comprehension.

The speech-language pathologist's role in improving verbal memory.

Because there are so many facets of verbal memory there are many possible areas of difficulty and many ways that the speech-language pathologist can intervene. The smallest building blocks of verbal memory are speech sound discrimination and phonological encoding. Thus, the suggestions provided in "The speech pathologist's role in improving listening and following directions" are also relevant here. However, verbal memory is also addressed at other levels.

One clear suggestion from memory research is that automaticity results from practice. Thus, the more opportunities a child has to use new information, the better. And for children with weakness in language processing even more practice will be needed than for children with normal language processing.

Researchers working with head-injured children have shown that they can retrain memory by teaching certain memory strategies. A speech-language pathologist can teach children to use these memory strategies which have been shown to be effective. They include: 1) chunking numbers into groups, 2) organizing information by category, 3) mediation through self-questioning, 4) using mnemonics such as rhymes, words or sentences (e.g., "Thirty days hath September . . ." for remembering which months have 30, 31 or 28 days; or "Every Good Boy Does Fine" for remembering EGBDF, the notes that correspond to the lines on the musical staff, 4) actively forming mental images, and 5) actively forming associations such as between a new face and that person's name. The eventual goal of therapy is for the patient to use the strategies spontaneously.

16

SUGGESTIONS FOR IMPROVING WORD RETRIEVAL

A word-retrieval or word-finding problem is one type of memory problem which is so specific and so commonly encountered that it is considered separately from other verbal memory problems.

External strategies: What parents and teachers can do to help.

Allow time. Give the LPP child extra time to retrieve words.

Help find the word. Ask questions like "What do you do with it?" or "Can you think of something else like it?". Encourage the child to think of another way to say what she means. Make some guesses and together you may be able to work it out.

Talk about words. When the word is found, or when introducing new vocabulary, talk about the features of the word. How does it sound? How does it look? What does it mean or have or do? Does it have other meanings? What words mean almost the same thing? What category does it fit into? What does it make you think of? Answering these questions helps the child develop many connections between words and their uses. These connections may later provide a variety of routes for accessing the stored word.

Encourage use of strategies. Let your LPP child work through the word-retrieval process out loud until he becomes an expert. "Do I know anything about how the word sounds?" "What category is it in?" "What does it go with?" "When and where did I last hear the word?" "Who says this word?", etc.

Internal strategies: What children can learn to do to help themselves.

Ask for time. Saying "Just give me a minute to think of the word" or even just raising your finger will let the listener know you are trying to think and give you a little more time to think.

Circumlocute. Try to express the same idea in another way, even if it takes longer and is not as efficient.

Use specific routes. Search out all possible clues about how the word sounds or what might make it come to mind. Do you know how the word starts, how long it is, anything about how it sounds? What other words or ideas does it go with? Can you picture someone saying it or remember where you last heard it? Figure out which route works best.

Relax. Sometimes the harder someone tries to find the word the more it remains hidden. Very often after the decision is made to skip it and figure out another way to express the idea, the desired word comes popping up as if by magic.

Practice. When you learn a new word practice saying it over and over. Use it as often as you can. The more you use a word, the easier it will be to retrieve it.

The speech-language pathologist's role in improving word retrieval.

There are at least two kinds of help the speech-language pathologist can give for word retrieval problems. There is research support for both methods. One is elaboration, or, increasing the amount of information that a child has about a word. This is thought to increase the number of connections between the word and other words and concepts in long term memory and thus provide more possible entry points to access the word. For best results this elaboration should include speech sound and visual information in addition to information about the meaning of the word.

The other effective technique is to teach retrieval strategies. These would include cuing by attributes or association such as beginning sound, category, gesture or synonym. The goal of this treatment is for the child to learn the cues that works best for him and to begin to cue himself.

Diane German points out that understanding the precise nature of the word-finding problem is essential to providing effective treatment. Does the child have trouble retrieving words she knows well? Is she accurate but slow at naming, or quick to give an inaccurate response? Is the problem worse for isolated naming or in conversation? In answering these and other specific questions the speech-language pathologist can best determine the exact treatment course.

In addition to elaborating semantic networks and learning self-cuing techniques, German recommends that speech-language pathologists teach children strategies for getting their message across using other words or descriptions. She feels that treatment should also train children to inhibit impulsive responses and to modify inappropriate verbalization (mazes) when searching for words.

17

SUGGESTIONS FOR IMPROVING ORGANIZATION OF LANGUAGE OUTPUT

External strategies: What parents and teachers can do to help.

Provide a relaxed atmosphere. When children are rushing to express their thoughts they tend to have more difficulty organizing ideas. Make it clear that you are interested in what they have to say and have plenty of time to listen. (Of course this is not always possible, but make sure that there are frequently times when it is).

Encourage expression. Encourage children to tell about their experiences and dreams and to tell or retell stories. Practice improves retrieval and organization.

Review main points. When a child's story becomes long and you begin to lose the train of thought, ask pertinent questions for clarification. Who was involved? What happened? etc. Say back the main points of the story as you understand them. This helps to make sure you are understanding and to keep the child's story focused.

Avoid putting children on the spot. For example, at family gatherings or other social situations, LPP children should not be asked to "say your ABC's" or "tell Aunt Nelly about your science project" (unless you know the child really wants to do this).

Take turns. During group discussions (including family dinner table conversation) make sure each participant has uninterrupted turns to speak.

Expect a response. When a child consistently responds "I don't know" or "nothing" to questions, help her to formulate a more appropriate answer by giving cues or asking different questions.

If you don't understand, say so. Even if it is more convenient to pretend you understood what a child said you should let him know that you did not. Otherwise more serious misunderstandings will ensue. You don't have to repeatedly say "What?" or "I didn't understand". You can say "I think you said ___", giving your best guess about what was said. Then the child has an opportunity to confirm or deny it. You may have to make quite a few guesses. This works well with young children and they love it when you make goofy guesses.

Internal strategies: What children can learn to do to help themselves

Pause. Take a moment to think and plan before speaking. Just a little extra time can improve organization by a lot.

Slow down speech rate. Slower speech is easier to understand *and* speaking more slowly allows more time for word retrieval and sentence organization.

Gain time. Speakers gain extra time in many ways. Saying "Let me think about that" or gesturing that you are thinking works fairly well. It is much more effective than repeating words or throwing in fillers such as "um", "like", "you know", or just talking aimlessly. These interferences are called mazes. They tend to confuse your listener and don't help get the point across.

The speech-language pathologist's role in improving organization of language output.

The speech-language pathologist can provide lots of help in this area. Frequently children who have trouble organizing sentences can benefit from treatment to improve their knowledge and use of certain grammatical constructions.

Especially notable in this regard are the problems many older LPP children have using subordinating conjunctions and relative pronouns. These structures are used to establish the relationship between two or more ideas forming one sentence. The resultant sentences are often quite long. Because of constraints on verbal memory, many LPP children do not learn to understand and use this type of sentence. It often helps to teach the use of these relational words in very short sentences. For example, "Unless it rains, we will be there" or "The dog, who is wet, is mine". Repeated practice using such subordinating conjunctions and relative pronouns in increasingly longer sentences will help these structures to be processed and used more automatically.

Speech-language pathologists can also teach strategies for organizing longer spoken passages. These would include giving descriptions or directions, reporting events and telling stories.

Descriptions and directions can be improved by helping children to focus on the most important attributes or most important landmarks to tell their listener. The speech-language pathologist can help children understand what information their listeners need most.

Children's narratives (stories and reports of events) can be improved by using certain organizing structures. Elementary school children can learn to effectively use Who, What, When, Where, Why, How as a format to organize information for written and spoken narratives.

In addition the speech-language pathologist can help children become aware of the use of mazes and train more appropriate speech behaviors. These could include speaking more slowly, pausing before beginning a sentence or asking the listener to wait.

18
A FINAL WORD

Each of the many ideas presented in the previous chapters has been found helpful for some children. Keeping in mind the language tasks that seem most difficult for your child will help you choose the best strategies to try. In doing this you will be helping your child make the first steps toward more effective communication.

One important aim of this book has been to empower parents and teachers by showing them how to recognize language processing problems and by giving them workable strategies for making a difference. Whether or not your child needs to receive further help from a speech and language pathologist, you can begin to implement appropriate strategies for better communication. These strategies can be used at home and at school. Changes you make are likely to benefit not only the LPP child, but everyone else in the home or school environment.

In addition to empowering parents and teachers, the goals of this book have been to define language processing problems, bring to light the fact that many children with LPP have not been adequately diagnosed and to convey, in simple terms, what is currently known about how language is processed and the problems which can occur during processing. I hope that I have succeeded in improving your understanding of language processing and how it relates to other language and learning problems.

Developing a better picture of the problems inherent in processing language gives us insight. It allows us to be more understanding and helpful when our children have problems with comprehension or expressing themselves. But it also sheds light on problems we sometimes find ourselves or other adults having with language. I hope that readers of this book will go forth with an awareness of the complexity of language, a willingness to make an effort to improve their communicative interactions, and a graceful tolerance for the slips and errors that are sometimes made by both children and adults in difficult speaking situations.

GLOSSARY

amplitude—the extent of vibratory movement, for example of a sound wave.

automaticity—the quality or state of being automatic.

bottom-up processes—processes that begin analyzing the most basic units and proceed to more complex units.

cochlea—spiral canal in the inner ear with hairlike organs which receive specific frequencies of sound.

coding—to put into the form of symbols or code. The sounds of spoken language, for example, take various forms or codes (waveforms, electrical and neural firing, etc.) from the time they are produced until they are understood.

cognition—intellectual process by which knowledge is gained about perceptions or ideas. The act or process of knowing, in the broadest sense.

communication—sharing of information by transmission and reception of signals.

cortex—the outer layer of gray matter of the brain that contains most of the higher nervous centers.

decoding—to identify the constituent significant elements of a message. For example, understanding an utterance or making the transition from written to auditory form of a word.

discourse—verbal interchange, the expression of ideas.

dyslexia—a disturbance of the ability to read.

expressive language—language output, either spoken or written. Evaluated in terms of size of vocabulary, length and complexity of utterances and grammatical correctness.

frequency—the number of repetitions of a periodic process over a unit of time (ex. sound waves per second).

garden path—the situation in which the beginning of a sentence contains a word sequence that causes us to develop a specific expectation about the meaning of the sentence which may be contradicted by the remainder of the sentence.

grammar—a branch of linguistics which deals with classes of words, their inflections and other means of indicating relationships with each other.

grammatical—correct as according to the grammar.

impairment—having diminished value or strength.

information processing—the steps involved in deriving meaningful content from sensory input and conveying meaning through an output mode.

language knowledge—what an individual knows about a language; words and rules stored in memory and available for use.

language processing—the acts of decoding, analyzing, retrieving from memory and organizing of language information which are required to understand or express an idea, either spoken or written.

language—a systematic means of communicating ideas or feelings by the use of conventionalized signs, sounds, gestures or marks having understood meaning.

language based learning disability—a disability which interferes with educational progress which is specific to language abilities, and which occurs in spite of normal nonverbal intelligence.

lexical access—the mental process of finding and matching sound sequences with their meanings and vice versa.

maze—a verbal tangle including repetitions, revisions, pauses or filler words which are not part of the final sentence being expressed.

memory span—the number of items an individual can routinely hold in short-term storage.

narrative—the telling of the particulars of an act, occurrence or course of events; a story.

neologism—a new word usage or expression; a made-up word.

neural connection—the connection made when cells in the

cortex of the brain (neurons) transmit electrical impulses to other neurons.

neurological—of or relating to the nervous system.

neurological disorder—a problem or defect affecting some aspect of the nervous system.

on-line language processing—language processing which takes place during listening, speaking or reading; as contrasted with understanding based on subsequent reflection.

otitis media—inflammation of the middle ear; may be accompanied by effusion of sticky fluid. Middle ear infection.

phoneme—the smallest unit of speech that distinguishes one utterance from another. In other words, the sounds from which words are made. The English alphabet is only a loose approximation of the actual set of phonemes. This is especially true for vowels since in English we use more than the 5 vowels in the alphabet. But consonant phonemes also differ from letters. For example, /s/ and /k/ are English phonemes. The letter "C" is not a phoneme but stands for /s/ or /k/ depending on the following vowel. The letter "S" is usually the phoneme /s/ at the beginning of a word, but can be the phoneme /z/ in the middle or at the end (think about the sounds in the word "causes"; both S's are produced as the phoneme /z/ and the initial phoneme is /k/.

phonology (phonological)—the set of phonemes of a language and the rules for combining them.

receptive language—language comprehension; evaluated in terms of number of words and complexity of grammatical structures understood.

semantic—of or relating to meaning in language.

short-term memory—static storage of information for a brief period.

specific language impairment—deficit in one or more areas of language ability in spite of normal non-verbal intelligence.

speech—the act of communicating or expressing thought in spoken words.

speech-language pathologist—professional responsible for evaluating and treating disorders of speech and language. In order to be fully qualified a speech-language pathologist should have a Certificate of Clinical Competence in Speech and Language (CCC-Sp) which requires at least a Masters Degree in Communication Disorders, passing of national boards and completion of a 9-month internship.

syntax—the orderly arrangement of words to show their mutual relations in the sentence.

top-down processes—processes that gather information by taking a broad view and making global inference.

tympanic membrane—the ear drum.

word retrieval—word-finding (see lexical access).

word—a sequence of phonemes with an arbitrarily defined meaning.

working memory—a dynamic, integrative system which manages both short-term storage and processing of information.

WORKS CITED

Baddeley, A. (1986) *Working Memory.* London: Oxford University Press.

Baddeley, A. (1982) *Your Memory, A User's Guide.* London: Penguin Books.

Baddeley, A., S. Gathercole and C. Papagno (1998) The phonological loop as a language learning device. *Psychological Review, 105*, 158-173.

Campbell, T. F., C. Dollaghan, H. Needleman and J. Janosky (1997) Reducing bias in language assessment: processing-dependent measures. *Journal of Speech, Language and Hearing Research, 40*, 519-525.

Dollaghan, C. and T.F. Campbell (1998) Nonword repetition and child language impairment. *Journal of Speech, Language and Hearing Research, 41*, 1136-1146.

Dollaghan, C., T. F. Campbell, J. Paradise, H. Feldman, J. Janosky and D. Pitcairn (1999) Maternal education and measures of early conversational speech and language. *Journal of Speech, Language and Hearing Research, 42*, 1432-1443.

Dollaghan, C. and N. Kaston (1986) A comprehension monitoring program for language-impaired children. *Journal of Speech and Hearing Disorders, 51*, 264-271.

Earobics [computer software] (1997) Cambridge, MA: Cognitive Concepts.

Fast ForWord [computer software] (1997) Berkeley, CA: Scientific Learning Corp.

Gathercole, S., C. Willis, A. Baddeley and H. Emslie (1994) The Children's Test of Nonword Repetition: A test of phonological working memory. *Memory, 2*, 103-127.

Gaulin, C. and T. F. Campbell (1994) A procedure for assessing verbal working memory in normal school-age children: Some preliminary data, *Perceptual and Motor Skills, 79,* 55-64.

German, D. (1989) *National College of Education Test of Word Finding (TWF).* Allen, TX: DLM Teaching Resources.

German, D. (1990) *National College of Education Test of Adolescent/Adult Word Finding (TAWF).* Allen, TX:DLM Teaching Resources.

German, D. (1992) Word-finding intervention for children and adolescents. *Topics in Language Disorders, 13,* 33-50.

Just, M. and P. Carpenter (1992) A capacity theory of comprehension: Individual differences in working memory. *Psychological Review, 99,* 122-149.

Loban, W. (1976) *Language Development: Kindergarten through Grade Twelve.* Urbana, IL: National Council of Teachers of English.

McKinnis, S. and M. Thompson (1999) Altered auditory input and language webs to improve language processing skills. *Language, Speech and Hearing in Schools, 30,* 302-310.

McNeil, M. and T. E. Prescott (1978) *The Revised Token Test.* Austin, TX: PRO-ED, Inc.

Miller, J. (1981) *Assessing Language Production in Children.* Austin, TX: PRO-ED, Inc.

Parente, R. and D. Herrmann (1996) Retraining memory strategies. *Topics in Language Disorders, 17,* 45-57.

Porch, B. E. (1979) *Porch Index of Communicative Ability in Children.* Palo Alto, CA: Consulting Psychologists Press.

Tallal, P. and M. Peircy (1974) Developmental aphasia: Rate of auditory processing and selective impairment of consonant perception. *Neuropsychologia, 12,* 83-93.

Tallal, P. and M. Peircy (1975) Developmental aphasia: The perception of brief vowels and extended stop consonants. *Neuropsychologia, 13,* 69-74.

Tallal, P., R. Sainburg, and T. Jernigan (1991) The neuropathology of developmental dysphasia: Behavioral, morphological, and physiological evidence for a pervasive temporal processing disorder. *Reading and Writing: An interdisciplinary Journal, 3,* 363-377.